MAIMONIDES

Medieval Modernist

MAIMONIDES

Medieval Modernist

by Fred Gladstone Bratton

BEACON PRESS · BOSTON

PREFACE

THERE ARE SOME whose warfare is hidden and internal but is nonetheless world-conquering, titanic. They are the heroes of thought and their battles are in the arena of the mind. Unlike the romantic figures of history, the warriors and rulers, there is little here of the glamorous or the scandalous to relate, no blood and thunder, *Sturm und Drang*. Consequently the heroes of the mind are given only a token recognition by historians and biographers. This, perhaps, is inevitable for it is still true—fortunately, one might add—that "goodness is not news," and the exemplary character does not make the headlines. Little is known of the private life of a Shakespeare, an Erasmus, a Spinoza. This too is as it should be, for in the long run it is in the great man's ideas that we are primarily interested, not his escapades. As someone has suggested, there is a larger perspective from which to view a genius than through the eyes of his valet. To deal with the flesh at the expense of the spirit in the case of a Byron or a Goethe may be intriguing, but a disproportionate attention to the private life of the hero may throw out of focus his creative ideas—and they, after all, are the important consideration.

Each generation needs to be reminded of those heroes of peace whose monuments are not in the public squares but in our cultural legacy. Their success was achieved not by subduing but by serving. Such a hero was Maimonides, who today is hardly more than a name, a personality overshadowed by his more dramatic contemporaries—Richard the Lion-hearted and Saladin the Magnanimous, Thomas à Becket and Thomas Aquinas; his voice smothered by the trumpeting of medieval warfare.

Maimonides has been grossly neglected by Christian writers in modern times. What few books have been written about him have been confined to Jewish authors who have, for the most part, written for Jewish readers and whose bibliographical references and textual terms are in Hebrew and therefore meaningless to Christian readers. So it may be that a non-Jewish approach to the life and teachings of the Rambam can bring to the subject a greater degree of objectivity and a wider perspective. At any rate, an appreciation of this universal thinker by a Gentile is long overdue. It is an index to the stature of Maimonides that the further he recedes in time, the larger his figure looms in the field of religious philosophy. But he has not received the recognition he deserves in the modern Christian world. While it contains nothing new factually for the informed Jewish reader, the present volume may serve partially to fill in a gap in Christian literature and to acquaint Gentiles with the thinking of the greatest Jewish philosopher next to Spinoza. My purpose, therefore, is to show the ways in which Maimonides has left the Christian world—as well as the Jewish—in his debt. Biographies of Maimonides in English have contained too little about his contemporaries and immediate predecessors in twelfth-century Moorish Spain, a defect which I have tried to remedy in the first chapter, for no great thinker can be divorced from his environment or his intellectual ancestry. I have also tried to appraise the influence of Maimonides on later European thought rather than merely on Christian Scholasticism. The last chapter is a brief discussion of the relevance of the

Maimonidean spirit to the problems of Christianity and Judaism today. To take the proper measure of a man, the competent historian must place himself sympathetically in the hero's time and presence, attaining if possible the feeling of immediacy, and at the same time stand off to view his subject from the perspective of the intervening years. Thus seeing the man with the bifocals of his era and ours, the biographer tries to render his verdict. His conclusion therefore must be twofold: what the hero meant to his own age and what niche he should hold in history.

Maimonides was the product of that radiant interlude in history, the Golden Age of Moorish Spain, a period which can be understood only as we go back to the early sixth century when Justinian, fearing the contamination of Christian theology by Greek thought, closed the philosophical schools of Athens. This fanatical edict of the emperor proved to be a blessing in disguise. It became a source of a new vitality as the Greek spirit found a new home in Arabia, Persia, Syria, and Egypt. Later the Moslem conquest carried this seed to Spain, where Arab and Jewish scholars with their new knowledge of Hellenism influenced the course of medieval and modern intellectual history.

Prior to the time of Averroës and Maimonides little was known of the philosophy of Aristotle. It was an irony of history that the ideas from which Justinian tried to protect Christianity in the sixth century became in the twelfth century, through the medium of Arab and Jewish scholars, the most potent force in medieval Christian thought. Chiefly responsible for this legacy to the Christian world was Maimonides, whose lasting contribution was the reconciliation of faith and reason and the substitution of a spiritual conception of God for the traditional anthropomorphic one.

But the influence of Maimonides in his own day was not confined to abstract thought. Possibly more important than his philosophy was his strengthening and unifying of world Judaism at a time when the Jewish community was on the verge of dissolution. It was around him that the Jews of the East and the West rallied in the face of possible extinction. Because of his leadership thousands of Jews returned to their own faith after they became, or were on the point of becoming, compulsory converts to Islam during the Almohavid rule. It was his teaching that became the guide to those who were perplexed because of the conflict between the new rationalism and the faith of their fathers. It was his clarification that led countless Jews through the tangled maze of the Talmud to a clearer comprehension of its bearing on their daily life. The tragic course of Judaism in the fourteenth and fifteenth centuries pushed the Maimonidean rationalism aside as the Jews in their desperation fled to the fanatical Cabbala for refuge. In times of crises most people resort to mystical fantasies and their beguiling illusions; but the seeds of reason blossomed again as Jewish scholarship helped prepare the way for the Enlightenment and nineteenth-century historical criticism.

The challenge of Maimonides to our day is his insistence on intelligence in religion. Dismayed by the present cults of nonreason and anti-intellectualism and by the cultural decline in mass media, the liberal-minded person will gratefully acknowledge his debt to this medieval modernist who, in a much darker and less tolerant age than this, had faith in man in spite of men, devoted himself to the life of reason, taught the paramount importance of moral integrity, and saw purpose in the universe.

Of course, the impact of Maimonides on our times can

only be one of spirit or attitude rather than method. He lived in the twelfth century. Profound though his works be, the erosive power of time has rendered much of his thought irrelevant for the twentieth century, but he still must be acknowledged as one of those titanic forces that helped to shape modernity by pointing may away from blind credulity to rationalism and supplying the criteria for change in theological and religious thinking.

Whoever attempts to write in the field of Jewish history must acknowledge the guidance of such contemporary authorities as Abram L. Sachar, Jacob B. Agus, Nahum N. Glatzer, Cecil Roth, and Salo W. Baron and earlier writers such as H. Graetz, Joseph Jacobs, and M. L. Margolis. For material related directly to the life and thought of Maimonides I am greatly indebted to the works of Solomon Zeitlin, David Yellin, Israel Abrahams, J. Münz, Salo W. Baron, and Isaac Husik. In this connection, mention must be made of the exhaustive two-volume symposium, *Moses ben Maimon: Sein Leben, Seine Werke, und Sein Einfluss,* edited by Jacob Guttmann and produced in commemoration of the seven-hundredth anniversary of the death of Maimonides. The bibliography has been limited to those volumes consulted in the preparation of this volume. Technical aspects of the Talmud and references to books in Hebrew have been avoided as having no interest to Christian readers. Dates are indicated thus: B.C.E. (Before Christian Era) and C.E. (Christian Era). The spelling of *Mishnah* should be explained: in Maimonides' own work it is *Mishneh Torah;* otherwise it is *Mishnah.*

I wish to thank the editorial staff of Beacon Press for valuable assistance in the preparation of the manuscript. My thanks also to Mrs. Frank A. Warren, who typed it.

Fred Gladstone Bratton

ACKNOWLEDGMENTS

I WISH TO THANK the following publishers for permission to quote from the works cited:

The Jewish Publication Society of America:
   Israel Zangwill (Trans. and Ed.), *Selected Religious Poems of Solomon ibn Gabirol*
   David Yellin and Israel Abrahams, *Maimonides*
   Isaac Husik, *A History of Medieval Jewish Philosophy*

Bloch Publishing Company:
   Solomon Zeitlin, *Maimonides: A Biography*

CONTENTS

MAIMONIDES

Medieval Modernist

CHAPTER ONE

The Golden Age

Moorish Spain

THE TWELFTH CENTURY in Europe was a turbulent and volcanic era, an age of paradox and extremes. Diabolical cruelty and lofty sentiments existed side by side, devilish imaginations and heavenly visions, inquisitorial tortures and saintly gentleness, blind credulity and heretical disbelief.

It was also the period in which the great cultural advance of the Abbasid rule in Bagdad shifted its center to Cordova in Spain which became the cradle of learning in the West. Here Arab physiology, hygiene, and medicine reached a highly advanced stage. While Christians were praying for miraculous cures, Moslem surgeons were performing miraculous operations. Arab mathematicians invented algebra and the decimal system; astronomers built observatories and made extended astronomical calculations; scientists invented paper. The Golden Age of Moorish Spain witnessed the building of magnificent mosques, palaces, schools, and libraries in Cordova, the Giralda and the Alcazar in Seville, and the incomparable Alhambra in Granada. It was in these three Andalusian cities that the Moorish genius reached its peak, each serving in turn as the artistic and intellectual capital of the West.

For the Arabs, with their desert background, the fragrant and fertile plain of Andalusia was a Mohammedan paradise, or became one in the hands of the caliphs. The Arabs brought to southern Spain the orange and the apricot, jasmine and the camellia, iron and leather work, silk and perfume. Cordova became the "Athens of the West." Its famous library had 400,000 volumes and its scholars were busy translating the Greek classics into Arabic. Poets and poetry filled the court. The city had steadily increased in size and grandeur until the middle of the eleventh century, when decline began to set in, and finally in 1236 it was captured by the Christians. At the height of the caliphate, according to Arab historians, Cordova had about 500,000 inhabitants, 300 mosques, 300 public baths, and twenty-one suburbs. Upper-class people had beautiful villas in the country. The houses in the city were patterned after Roman homes with interior courtyards and walled gardens. The gay and opulent life in the palace of Abd al-Rahman III was maintained on the top of a stratified order of society, a facade behind which was a world of violence and intrigue.

Abd al-Rahman's greatest undertaking was the building of the famous mosque at Cordova. It had been in the process of construction for several centuries but the major renovation and extension took place during his reign (929–961). Because of the large space to be roofed and the weight to be borne it was decided to construct double arches. These horseshoe arches, inspired undoubtedly by the Roman aqueduct and resting on slender columns, produced a magnificent fan effect. Under later caliphs, cupolas and domes, floral motifs and Byzantine mosaics, were added, giving the structure a more sumptuous Oriental look. The carved ceilings were of cypress, gold, and mother-of-pearl; the walls of marble and gold mosaics. There were gardens with fountains and groves with thousands of pomegranate and orange trees.

To the Moors, beauty and truth were equal. They joined the artistic and the scientific in perfect harmony. Religion was not the ascetic, fearful thing of medieval Christianity. It was a joyous and positive expression of the soul. It is in the palaces and mosques that one can appreciate the manner in which the Arab superimposed the aesthetic upon the utilitarian. In the arches and arabesques, geometrical precision is wedded to spiritual ecstasy, logic to insight. Mathematical design creates the feeling of infinity as the eye follows on ceiling and wall the abstract symbolism which has no beginning or end. The Koran forbade the Arabs to represent any living creatures in painting, sculpture, or relief. But they found a way to picture the spirit. The unending symmetrical design of Arabic characters becomes the visible expression of the spirit of God. Standing in the forest of marble, porphyry, and alabaster columns in the Cordovan mosque, 850 of them, one is lost in infinity. Here is the spiritual essence geometrically demonstrated. Thus did the Arabs recognize the equal importance of logic and insight, science and religion, as we shall later see in their profound respect for the Greek rationalism along with their Moslem monotheism.

The conquest of Spain by the Moors began in 711. Their greatest political unity was achieved under the caliphate of Cordova, which fell at the end of the twelfth century to be split up into faction-kingdoms throughout Andalusia. In 1492 Ferdinand and Isabella drove the Moors out of Granada, the last Moslem stronghold in the West. Some remained but were finally expelled by Philip III in the seventeenth century. The Arab spirit in art and architecture, philosophy and medicine had made its mark, however, and profoundly influenced such widespread movements as Catholic Scholasticism, Italian poetry, and Jewish philosophy. The monuments of Andalusia became a composite of Arab and Gothic architecture as the Christian kings converted mosques into cathedrals and minarets into bell towers. Today the two forms are intermingled.

The population of southern Spain also coalesced in blood, language, and religion. Many Moslems knew Latin; many Jews knew Arabic, in fact, adopted it as their vernacular. Arabic tended to replace Hebrew in secular writing, with the result that Jewish literature for several centuries appeared in both Hebrew and Arabic.

Medieval philosophers were greatly concerned with Greek thought, especially Aristotelianism, having been introduced to it originally by the Nestorians, the liberals of early Christianity. They were in a larger way drawn into the persistent philosophical and theological controversies that stirred the ancient Greeks, and it is in their discussion of these problems that they exerted a permanent influence on medieval scholasticism. The Christian church in Spain had withdrawn not only from life itself but also from abstract thought, with the result that invading Islam became its tutor. Earlier Arab philosophy was colored by the Neoplatonism of Plotinus. One representative of this school was Avicenna (980–1037), who was known for his medical knowledge as much as for his theology. His works were translated into Latin and became an integral part of the scholastic tradition as taught by Albertus Magnus. Avicenna's cosmic philosophy was a combination of Gnostic and Neoplatonic elements.

The most important Arab philosopher of the twelfth century was Averroës (1126–1198) of Cordova. Like practically all of the Jewish and Moorish scholars of that period, Averroës studied and practiced medicine, but it is his philosophical writings for which he is known. He is considered the greatest of medieval Moslem writers and one of the most influential thinkers in western history. His independent attitude brought on the hostility of orthodox Moslems who claimed that he had become a Jew. It is true that his writing carried more weight with Jewish thinkers from the twelfth century onward than any other Islamic philosopher. He was ostracized and his books were burned at the order of the Moslem rulers. The theologians succeeded in having him accused of heresy and apostasy to Judaism. He was banished from Cordova and went to Morocco, where he spent his later life.

The teaching of Averroës that precipitated the greatest opposition was his semi-evolutionary theory concerning the creation of the world. He held that creation was a continuous process, a growth, rather than a sudden making of the world by fiat. The creation is a constantly changing development, each new form coming from a previous one. This revolutionary idea was clearly contradictory to the traditional view of Christianity, Islam, and Judaism. Another unorthodox position held by Averroës was his apparent disbelief in the doctrine of the resurrection. He publicly denied such disbelief but it is nevertheless implied in his teaching about the soul and the intellect. The soul, he said, is immortal only insofar as it is a part of the Divine Reason or Universal Intellect. In his interpretation of Aristotle, Averroës distinguished between faith and reason, a distinction that led his followers to attribute to him the idea of a "twofold truth," namely, that faith and reason are mutually exclusive and that where philosophy conflicts with religion, the former is to be followed. In this conclusion his disciples may have confused his commentary on Aristotle with his own beliefs. Be that as it may, Averroës was regarded by some Christian bishops as the father of free thought and unbelief. It is probably nearer the truth to say that Averroës, like Aquinas, was simply trying to reconcile reason and faith. In that attempt both regarded the rationalism of the Greeks as highly important but they did not reject the idea of revealed religion. Perhaps it can be said that Averroës was more critical of literalism than Aquinas and at times did question the allegorical interpretations of obvious untruths in the Koran. He insisted that uniformity of interpretation is impossible. Here he resorted to a compromise (still proposed by some scholars) in saying that the ignorant mass of people should follow the text literally but the philosopher could view it in the light of reason and make his own interpretation. It must be concluded, however, that, although Averroës was ahead of his contemporaries in his rationalism, he has too much in common with Aquinas to warrant the assertion that he was a free thinker in the modern sense of the word.

The question of free will was the chief theme for discussion in Moorish Spain, and those who held that God could not overrule man's power of choice or predetermine man's actions came to be known as Mu'tazila or Secessionists, a name which was subsequently used to designate any who departed from the traditional attitude toward the Koran or who expressed liberal views. The Mu'tazilite position on free will arose from the fundamental idea of the divine righteousness, a principle which is inherent in the Hebrew concept *Zedeq*.[1] Even more significant for the cause of liberal thought was their belief that no theology should be above rational inquiry, that it was not enough merely to accept a dogma on faith as the word of God. The Mu'tazilites insisted that Islamic philosophy be grounded on logic and not on authority. They rejected all forms of anthropomorphism in reference to Deity and regarded the attribution to God of such personal qualities as knowledge, will, and feeling as polytheistic.

Eventually the Mu'tazilite teaching was suppressed by the government which made belief in the Koran compulsory.

[1] See also the Egyptian *maat*—order, cosmic rightness, truth.

8

But in spite of the resurgence of orthodoxy, concessions had to be made to this progressive group. A new speculative approach to theology was admitted in order to bring the faith of the fathers in line with rational thought. This movement was called *Kalam*, a form of Moslem scholasticism, and its two representatives were Abu al-Hassan al-Ashari and Abu al-Mansur al-Maturidi. In the long run, this was, like the Thomistic system, not much more than a method of rationalizing orthodoxy.

Jewish Scholasticism

The necessity of harmonizing revelation and reason, mysticism and empiricism, belief and knowledge, found expression also in Spanish Jewry in the same period. For Jewish orthodoxy, the Torah and the Talmud, representing the written and oral word of God, were equally inspired, infallible, and authoritative; but for the rationalist, the testimony of the Bible was ambiguous and at times contradictory. It could be quoted on either side of the questions of authority versus private inquiry, determinism versus freedom. The Bible, moreover, was inconsistent in its teachings on ethics, teleology, the nature of God, and God's relation to man. It appeared therefore to be incumbent upon the more progressive thinkers among the Jews to study philosophy and science in order to make a more intelligible interpretation, one that was consonant with reason and the facts of life and history.

The background of this new approach in Judaism was essentially Greek and started with the spread of Hellenism which followed in the wake of Alexander's conquest. Taking root in Alexandria, Mesopotamia, and Syria, Greek literature, art, science, and medicine were taught by the Monophysite Christians and the Nestorians. When the Near East became

Moslem, the Syrians became the chief transmitters of Greek learning, translating Hippocrates, Galen, Euclid, Archimedes, and Aristotle into Arabic. In Mesopotamia the Arabs had developed schools of philosophy and medicine and later brought their knowledge to western Europe. Thus it came about that Jewish scholars of the eleventh and twelfth centuries were heir to this body of Greek and Arabic learning.

Because of Islamic influence, the chief ingredient in Jewish thought was Aristotelianism, a system which gave to Judaism —at least to its leading thinkers—a more speculative turn. Biblical theology was purely ethical. There was no abstract analysis of the essence of created things, the nature of nature. Aristotle delved into the world of elements that made up the universe, both the seen and the unseen, concepts as well as things. His genius was classification and that led to logic. He discussed the relation of change to motion, form to matter, mind to body. All the problems of God, man, and the universe comprised his province. The distinctive element in his moral philosophy was the concept of the "golden mean," nothing to excess, perspective in all things. This stream of thought brought to Judaism a new diversity and greater dimensions.

The dualism of Aristotle (spirit and matter) was supplemented by the monism of Plotinus as a further influence on medieval Jewish thinking. The Neoplatonic philosophy amounted almost to pantheism in relating everything to God, the world ground, and primal cause. It shared with Gnosticism the belief that God is unknowable, that matter is the origin of evil, and that the universe consists of emanations from God.

Much of the Neoplatonic-Aristotelian influence came into Jewish philosophy by way of the tenth-century Moslem order called the Brethren of Purity. Their fifty-one treatises synthesized the scientific approach of Aristotle and the mysticism of Plotinus. A further influence in this direction came from Avicenna and Averroës, Spanish-Arabian philosophers whom we have already mentioned.

We are prepared then to find Jewish medieval thought in Spain taking one or all of three forms: Kalamism, Aristotelianism, and Neoplatonism. On the background of Greek rationalism on the one hand and biblical-Talmudic revelation on the other, we can expect with few exceptions an acceptance of philosophy and logic as a supplement to, and correction of, revealed religion. Truth may be found subjectively by human insight and reason and also by empirical and historical evidence. Of course, we cannot suppose that these thinkers rose above their times, anticipating nineteenth- and twentieth-century thought. There has never been a genius in any field who was not a child of his own age to a greater or less degree. These Jewish philosophers were unable, lacking the insight or courage, to follow the implications of their rational outlook to its logical conclusion—an observation, it might be added, even more applicable to modern theologians whose liberalism in religious philosophy is allowed to go just so far and no farther. They could hardly be expected to transcend the geocentric and ethnocentric point of view of their time. For that matter, the leading Christian thinkers of today are not much different. In spite of all our new knowledge of the universe, they refuse to define God as a cosmic force but continue to follow the parochial conception of God as creator of this planet only, a Deity concerned only with the Christian religion as an exclusive revelation through Jesus Christ who is his son and savior of the world.

The importance of the Spanish Jews is that they did arrive at a less particularistic and more universal conception of

God. They saved Judaism for the nineteenth and twentieth centuries and went a long way toward making it consonant with secular learning and not contradictory to it. They were the transmitters of Hellenism to the West. They were discussing Plato and Aristotle, Epictetus and Plotinus, the nature of God and man, good and evil, freedom and authority, while Christian Europe, for the most part, was stagnating in intellectual barbarism. Medieval Jewry was the intermediary between East and West and may be considered to constitute the longest cultural period in the history of Europe excepting classical Greece.

The centers of Jewish learning prior to the eleventh century were in Egypt and Babylonia. Babylonian Jewry could boast of its great institutions of higher learning at Sura and Pumbeditha. The Academies, as they were called, were attended not only by scholars, but were open at certain periods in the year to all who cared to take advantage of the educational opportunities. They were forerunners of our adult education and university-extension programs. As a result of this widespread education the scholar became the most respected man in the community. The head of the Academy occupied the highest position of leadership and was called Gaon, a title of great distinction. As the successors of the Talmudic sages, the Geonim attracted students from many countries and instructed them in the minutiae of postbiblical traditions.

Toward the end of the Gaonic or Babylonian period there were two movements which deserve our special attention: one, conservative; the other, liberal. Karaism, founded by Anan ben David in 750 and originating in Bagdad, was a revolt directed against Rabbinism and the Talmud, and aimed at restoring the Bible to its position as the sole authority in Judaism. The name Karaites derives from their strict adherence to the written word of the Bible unaccompanied by the pedantic intricacies of interpretation. This was reminiscent of the teaching of the Sadducees, who by the second century had disappeared. As a purist movement Karaism no doubt appealed to many intelligent people to whom the Talmud represented confusion worse confounded, a cumbersome conglomeration of hairsplitting legislation that required a legal mind to fathom. Ironically, the freedom gained from the restrictions of Talmudic dietary and ritualistic practices was counterbalanced by their greater fidelity to the Mosaic code, which, when literally followed, produced many inconveniences in daily life. The movement spread rapidly to Egypt, Persia, Palestine, and Spain, reaching its greatest development in the twelfth century. Thereafter it lost its influence, having shown itself to be too static for a changing world. It did, however, have the beneficial effect of instigating new biblical studies. It further encouraged individual interpretation of the Scripture. This also was a mixed good, for, while the spirit of individual inquiry was an admirable idea, it prevented the movement from becoming unified. With each person acting as his own authority on the Bible, chaos resulted. Karaism gradually disintegrated but not without demonstrating that Rabbinism, like all religious movements, could profit by occasional revolts.[2]

Of much greater importance for the history of the Jewish religion in general and biblical interpretation in particular was Gaon Saadia (892–942). He was born in Egypt and received a good education in Islamic and Talmudic literature. After extended periods in Palestine and Syria, he settled in Babylonia, where he became head of the Academy at Sura.

---

[2] A remnant of the Karaite movement, numbering some ten or twelve thousand persons, exists today, chiefly in Russia.

Under his direction this school became the most important center of learning in the Near East.

As a reaction to Islamic theology, Saadia undertook a thoroughgoing clarification of Judaism in his chief work, *Beliefs and Opinions*. In this volume he attempted to interpret Judaism in the light of scientific and philosophical criteria. His harmonizing of reason and revelation set the pace for all later rationalistic philosophers from Gabirol to Maimonides. He maintained that the world was created in time and that God the Creator was unified, incorporeal, and without attributes of any kind. To make God a trinity, he argued, is to attribute to him corporeality and to fall prey to anthropomorphism. As for man, Saadia held clearly to the doctrine of free will. Man has choice; his life is not predetermined. Truth, he says, is arrived at by three universal methods: the senses, judgment, and logical inference; his view of Scripture, however, compelled him to add revelation as a fourth source of authority.

Saadia's translation of the Bible into Arabic and his commentary on it prepared the way for the study of Hebrew grammar and philology. His biblical exegesis assumed a more rationalistic spirit than had ever been known before. He was the first Jew to approach the Bible critically and historically, a method continued by Rabbi Isaac of Toledo, who observed that Genesis 36:31 ("before there reigned any king over Israel") could have been written only after the accession of Saul as king, thus implying the non-Mosaic authorship of at least that part of the Pentateuch. Much of Saadia's biblical studies must be seen as a reaction to Karaism and were, along with the disunity of that movement, the chief reason for its dissolution. He showed that the Karaites, like most revolts, by developing a set of impractical traditions of their own, had brought about the very thing they set out to abolish. His anti-Karaite polemics succeeded in removing the threat of the movement and restored Talmudic supremacy in Judaism.

Mention must be made in passing of Isaac Israeli (855–955), a contemporary of Saadia, who, in addition to the distinction of living for a century, was famous as a physician. It was, in fact, only as a medical authority that Maimonides had any esteem for him. He was born in Egypt and went from there to Kairuan where he served several Fatimid caliphs as court physician. Two of his philosophical writings survive: *On Definitions*, a list of terms later used by Christian Scholastics, and *On Elements*, an exposition of Aristotelian physics. He was chiefly a compiler, not concerned with Jewish thought as it touched upon the Bible, but was rather an eclectic, drawing upon Aristotle and Plotinus. He was one of the first Babylonian Jews to introduce Greek ideas to medieval Judaism.

At the end of the ninth century the Jewish intellectual arena shifted from Babylonia to Spain with the accession of the tolerant and scholarly Abd al-Rahman III as caliph of Cordova. He was a patron of art and learning and as Abram L. Sachar remarks, "prized a good poem above a brave deed in battle." [3] His was a glorious reign in which Jewish learning, religious and scientific, was encouraged. The period from 900 to 1200 in Spain was perhaps the happiest one in Jewish history. The congenial attitude of the Spanish rulers, providing a stimulating environment, and the complete absence of persecution allowed the Jewish genius in medicine, philosophy, and poetry to flourish unhindered in the most prosperous country in Europe. It was in such a cultural setting

[3] Abram L. Sachar, *A History of the Jews* (New York, Alfred A. Knopf, Inc., 1953), p. 169.

that the Jews became the great intermediaries between the Arabic civilization and the Christian world and also made their own original contribution to western civilization.

This ascendancy of Cordova as the center of Jewish learning was given a great impetus by the caliph's Jewish advisers, Hasdai ibn Shaprut and Moses ben Enoch. Hasdai was the court physician as well as the official adviser in matters of state. He founded the Academy at Cordova, and Moses ben Enoch became its head.

Gabirol

The first prominent philosopher among the Spanish Jews was Solomon ibn Gabirol, known also as Avicebron (1021–1058). With him starts the golden era of Jewish literature. Gabirol was one of the truly great poets of medieval Judaism and wrote in flawless Hebrew. Many of his poems were incorporated into the liturgical literature of the synagogue. Their lyric and devotional quality can be appreciated in the following example:

AT THE DAWN

At the dawn I seek thee
Rock and refuge tried,
In due service speak thee
Morn and eventide.

'Neath thy greatness shrinking,
Stand I sore afraid,
All my secret thinking
Bare before thee laid.

Little to thy glory
Heart or tongue can do;
Small remains the story,
Add we spirit too.

Yet since man's praises ringing
May seem good to thee,
I will praise thee singing
While thy breath's in me.[4]

Gabirol's most important philosophical work was *Fountain of Life*, which helped to introduce Neoplatonic thought to Moslem Spain and also greatly influenced the Christian Scholastics. It was unfavorably received by the Jews because it was written originally in Arabic and then translated into Latin at the suggestion of the archbishop of Toledo. Furthermore, there was no reference to the Bible or the Talmud and the content was purely speculative rather than religious. Consequently Gabirol's name was forgotten for a long time except as a poet. The Scholastics who studied the *Fons Vitae* had no idea that the author was a Jew. Some thought he was a Moslem; others, a Christian. On the other hand, Gabirol, as a thoroughgoing monotheist, wrote distinctly in line with the Jewish tradition, saying that no quality should be attributed to God that would detract from his unity or uniqueness. The liberal spirit of his *Fountain of Life* is attested by the fact that it was denounced by Thomas Aquinas and supported by Duns Scotus. It was not until the middle of the nineteenth century that the mysterious Avicebron was known to be the Jewish poet Gabirol.

Halevi

If Averroës and Gabirol sided with reason as against revelation, Judah Halevi (1085–1140) took the reverse position. Philosophy with him was entirely inadequate as a source of

[4] *Selected Religious Poems of Solomon Ibn Gabirol,* Israel Davidson, ed., trans. by Israel Zangwill (Philadelphia, The Jewish Publication Society of America, 1923), p. 2.

truth and wisdom. It was incapable of teaching the profound truths about God and man.

Halevi lived in Toledo when that city was taken by Alfonso VI. The Christian king followed the tolerant policy of his predecessor, the Moslem emir, and treated the Jews kindly. As a poet, Halevi ranks with Gabirol, but like so many other Moslem and Jewish leaders of the period, he earned his living by practicing medicine. For a few years he lived in Cordova, which had already entered its period of decline and was ruled at the time by fanatical Moslem religionists. Here he wrote a number of poems and through them became famous as a strong Zionist. The following is a typical expression of his hope for the restoration of the Jewish national life in Palestine.

MY HEART IS IN THE EAST

My heart is in the East, and I in the uttermost West—
How can I find savor in food? How shall it be sweet to me?
How shall I render my vows and my bonds, while yet
Zion lieth beneath the fetter of Edom, and I in Arab chains?
A light thing would it seem to me to leave all the good
    things of Spain—
Seeing how precious in mine eyes to hold the dust of the
    desolate sanctuary.[5]

In 1140 Halevi left Spain for Palestine, but his ship was blown off its course and he landed at Alexandria. From there he went to Cairo. Despite the entreaties of his devoted friends to stay in Egypt, he continued his journey. History tells of his reaching Damascus but nothing is certain beyond that point. Legend has it that he was killed as he approached the gates of Jerusalem.

[5] Leon Feuer, *Jewish Literature Since the Bible*, Book One (Cincinnati, The Union of American Hebrew Congregations, 1942), p. 96.

rationalize or explain away a miracle that he knew could not be accepted as fact, but generally he rejected allegory along with some of the Midrashic interpretation in favor of his own historical and common-sense method. His biblical exegesis was neither complete nor consistent but he did form the connecting link between the ancient and modern world of biblical scholarship. His masterly knowledge of Hebrew enabled him to clarify many obscure passages and render the original text more accurately.

Of verbal inspiration in the Bible ibn Ezra would have none, and the miraculous element played no significant role as far as he was concerned. He could not believe that biblical writers predicted later events. The prophets for him were forthtellers, not foretellers. Commenting on Genesis 12:6 ("and the Canaanite was then in the land"), he observed that such a passage was obviously post-Mosaic. It was clear to him, in view of the retrospective language of Genesis concerning the Mosaic and Canaanite periods, that the Pentateuch in its entirety could not be attributed to Moses. The recognition of various recensions of the Decalogue and linguistic differences within the Pentateuch confirmed his doubt of Mosaic authorship. He was one of the first to detect a second authorship in Isaiah, a hand that was undoubtedly postexilic, for the references to Cyrus as the deliverer of the Jews could hardly have been written by the eighth-century Isaiah! He also ventured the suggestion that the latter part of II Samuel was of different authorship from the first part. All these observations, however, were couched in language indicating that he was afraid of offending orthodoxy.[7] Thus, instead of desig-

[7] It is surprising how slow scholars are, even to this day, in accepting the findings of historical criticism regarding the Pentateuch.

nating the Garden of Eden, the Tree of Knowledge, and the Cherubim as unhistorical, he suggests that they are symbols or representations of ethical and spiritual ideas. At times he becomes enigmatic in his symbolic use of numbers in the Scripture. This was neither the first nor the last attempt to rationalize by way of allegory. It was the method of the earlier Alexandrian school and is also typical of Neo-Orthodoxy and Biblical Theology and other conservative groups of our own day.

Ibn Ezra was born in Toledo. He traveled to Rome, Egypt, Morocco, and in 1158 arrived in London. While there he wrote *The Foundation of Religion,* which describes Jewish learning in twelfth-century England. Several of his mathematical works were translated into Latin. In addition to mathematics, he wrote voluminously on astronomy, philosophy, medicine, and Hebrew grammar. As a poet, he ranks next to Halevi, and much of his poetry found its way into the Jewish liturgical literature. The following poem, expressing the ubiquity of God as cosmic consciousness is reminiscent of the Psalms, Wordsworth, and Tennyson.

> Wheresoe'er I turn my eyes,
> Around on earth or toward the skies,
> I see thee in the starry field,
> I see thee in the harvest's yield,
> In every breath, in every sound,
> An echo of thy name is found.
>
> The blade of grass, the simple flower,
> Bear witness to thy matchless power.
> My every thought, eternal God of Heaven,
> Ascends to Thee, to whom all praise is given.[8]

[8] From Joseph Friedlander, *Standard Book of Jewish Verse* (New York, Dodd, Mead and Co., 1917).

To enter into the philosophical system of ibn Ezra would only be a recapitulation of that of his predecessors—a combination of Aristotle and Neoplatonism—with the difference that in his writings there is found a more critical and historical point of view. Also from ibn Ezra to Maimonides and later to Spinoza a greater place is given to the ethical criterion and the life of reason.

Ibrihim ibn Daud

Ibn Daud (1090–1165) is best known as a translator of Arabic. He was born in Toledo five years after the city fell into the hands of the Christians. He was converted to Christianity and acquired an expert knowledge of Latin. In trilingual Spain, Jewish scholars were known by two or three names. As a Spaniard he was originally Johannes Hispalensis; his Arabic name was Ibrihim ibn Daud (Hebrew: Abraham ben David) but the Schoolmen, with whom he became closely associated, called him Avendeath.

Ibn Daud's translation of Avicenna's *On the Soul* into Spanish (subsequently translated into Latin by Dominicus Gundissalinus, Archbishop of Segovia) exerted a great influence in the West, as did his translation of Avicebron's *Fountain of Life*. He translated from the Arabic numerous astronomical and mathematical works, thus making available for the Latin West a valuable library of Eastern learning. One of his translations into Latin, the *Secretum Secretorum*, was reproduced in hundreds of manuscripts in many languages and was frequently published after the invention of printing. Perhaps his most important translation was that of the writings of the Persian Muhammed ibn Musa al-Kwarizmi (ninth century). In this work the Arabic numerals in order of their value appear for the first time, displacing the old Latin numerals. Eventually, Western mathematics was built upon this system of notation.

As a philosopher, ibn Daud was quite the antithesis of Halevi, the mystical poet and conservative. Ibn Daud was nothing if not scientific and analytical. He continued the earlier attempt to harmonize Aristotelianism with Judaism, Hellenic rationalism with Hebraic revelation. These two disparate approaches to truth can never be completely harmonized, but the Spanish Jews from Gabirol to Maimonides did much to extricate religion from the grip of superstition and blind credulity and went a long way toward the liberal way of life. Philosophy cannot stop with Aristotle and religion cannot rest with divine revelation. Religion is man's upward reach to the skies; it is something that belongs to human nature, a groping and a grasping for the divine in life, a search for the ultimate, the eternal, the ideal, the source of all reality. The Bible and the Talmud are not the sole repositories of divine truth; else God is not a universal Being but a respecter of persons, partial to one people.

With ibn Daud, Neoplatonism fades into the background and Aristotle alone occupies the throne of philosophy. On the basis of Aristotelian logic, ibn Daud held to the incorporeal and eternal nature of God. As for man and the problem of will, he asserted that man is free to choose between good and evil and he also makes allowance for chance. Man must cooperate with the laws of nature and accept them. While there are some things that are determined by God, there are also contingencies by reason of natural causation, accident, or human choice. Man's ideal is happiness and that is achieved through moral choices, family devotion, and public integrity. The Golden Mean in all things is the goal to be sought. Thus we see in the rational and ethical emphasis of ibn Daud an anticipation of Maimonides and the modern temper.[9]

We have in this chapter described the cultural milieu of twelfth-century Spain—the Golden Age of Arab-Jewish learning—and the thinking of the leading Jewish scholars of that period. The appearance of this group of Jewish sages, three centuries before the intellectual revolution of Europe in the Renaissance, was a singular phenomenon. Such clusters of genius, of course, have arisen at several junctures of history: the Periclean, the Elizabethan, the Florentine, and the Concord circles. The flowering of Arab-Jewish learning was a link between the Golden Age of Greece and its rebirth in Italy in the fifteenth century. In an otherwise dark age these medieval thinkers led man to a more profound and more comprehensive conception of his relation to God, other men, and the cosmos. They had their limitations; their grasp of truth was only partial; yet they were prophets and indicated, as Emerson wrote, "to lesser minds the paths they must pursue." They created an intellectual climate that prepared the way for Descartes, Bacon, and Spinoza.

The greatest of them all, the culmination of Jewish philosophy, and the most brilliant star in the firmament of medi-

[9] The Jewish scholars Levi ben Gerson, or Gersonides (1288–1344), and Hasdai ben Abraham Crescas (1340–1410) do not lie within the scope of our study, the former being a Frenchman and the latter, living in a later period. Gersonides' chief contribution was his refutation of the homocentric theory that heavenly bodies move around the same center, a position which makes him partially a forerunner of Copernicus. Crescas was the first thinker to see Judaism in a nonspeculative way, completely independent of rationalism and Aristotelianism. He was therefore opposed to Gerson and Maimonides in his anti-intellectual attitude.

eval Jewry, was Moses ben Maimon (1135–1204), also known as Maimonides, Maimuni, or Rambam.[10]

The versatile mind of Maimonides encompassed every aspect of biblical and Talmudic literature, Greek philosophy, and Arabic science. He was a practicing physician and wrote profusely on medical theory. He was an authority on mathematics and astronomy. His achievement was to clarify the Hebrew religion for all time by a simplification of the complex Talmudic literature, to incorporate the Greek ideal of beauty and truth into Hebrew thought, and to reestablish Judaism on its prophetic, ethical foundation of justice and righteousness. In Maimonides is found the perfect synthesis of Greek rationalism and Hebrew piety. He was, as Henry T. Schnittkind writes, "the Hebrew Aristotle." But his religious philosophy was not merely speculative. All of his writings, in fact, were related to the practical aspects of life and to the needs of the time.

This utilitarian outlook influenced Maimonides' literary style to no small degree. Even his metaphysical writings were governed by the teleological principle; that is, he wrote at all times with a specific end in view, discarding all tangential elements. He regarded language as a means to an end, as a transmitter of ideas; and for him the prime ingredient of style was clarity rather than beauty. He shunned the poetic as detrimental to his strictly ethical emphasis. His insistence on clarity and conciseness compels the reader to concentrate on one cardinal idea. Subordinate material is necessary only as it bears on the main point. Regarding economy of words, he writes: "Those who study my works know that I always

[10] Maimonides is the Greek for the son of Maimon. Rambam is a nickname formed from the initials of Rabbi Moshe ben Maimon. His Arabic name was Abu Imran Musa ibn Maimun ibn Abdallah.

strive to avoid all polemical argument and lengthy discussion. If I were able to condense the whole Talmud into one page, I assuredly would not extend it to two." But brevity alone does not make for literary style. Individuality, taste, wit, and felicity of expression are necessary qualities, and these are not lacking in Maimonides' writings. One of his rhetorical methods was the use of metaphor and analogy. The saying that "one picture is worth a thousand words" is well illustrated in his frequent and masterful use of the form of comparison in which the simple parallelism illuminates the idea much more effectively than pages of abstract discussion. Along with the illustrative method Maimonides used a vigorous and at times caustic language which, without resorting to vulgarities, drove home his point in a convincing manner.

He had no interest in knowledge for its own sake.[11] By his definition religion was nothing if not ethical and activistic; it was not merely a personal virtue or passive ecstasy, but a constant expression of unselfish goodwill.

His combined devotion to the life of reason and his concept of God as Cosmic Mind made him the precursor of Spinoza and Einstein. His chief work, *The Guide for the Perplexed*, influenced all later Jewish and Christian thought. In an age of fanaticism and superstition he was the prophet of reason. In the midst of a world gone mad with holy wars he was the prophet of peace and sanity. He was, in short, a medieval modernist.

[11] See Michael Guttmann, "Maimonides als Dezisor" in *Moses ben Maimon: Sein Leben, Seine Werke, und Sein Einfluss*, Jacob Guttmann, ed. (Leipzig, Buchhandlung Gustav Fock, 1908–1914), Vol. 2, p. 306. "Die Veranlassung zum Schreiben entspringt nicht rein wissenschaftlichen Motiven, sondern Zeitbedürfnisse sind es, die Maimonides zu befriedigen, tiefempfundene Lücken, die er auszufüllen sucht."

CHAPTER TWO

The Wandering Jew

Bride of Andalusia

THE VISITOR TO CAIRO TODAY can, if he takes the pains, find his way through the old quarter of the city to a house of prayer called the Synagogue of Maimonides. In it an eternal light burns in memory of the great Rambam. Here, it is said, his body lay in repose for a week before being carried to the Holy Land for burial. As the funeral procession wended its way across the desert, legend has it, a band of Bedouins attacked the caravan. When they learned whose body it was they were about to violate they fell to the ground and begged forgiveness. Then they formed a bodyguard and accompanied the cortège to the Holy Land. The "Second Moses" was leaving the land of Egypt for Canaan, the home of the prophets.

The veneration in which Maimonides was held by his would-be assailants was shared alike by Arabs, Jews, and Christians throughout the Near East and Europe. The reason was that he had spent his life in behalf of others as physician, teacher, interpreter, and guide.

The life that came to an end in Cairo started in Cordova, Spain, in 1135. By that time civil war and Christian aggression had reduced the power and grandeur of Andalusia and the days of Moslem rule were numbered. But the Moorish city on the banks of the Guadalquivir was still the beautiful "Bride of Andalusia," the Bagdad of Europe, with its gardens, fountains, palaces, and mosques. It was still the intellectual and cultural capital of Spain. The young Moses wandered through

the interminable jasper and marble halls of the Great Mosque
of Abd al-Rahman III, absorbing the beauty and the spiritual
overtones of the arches and arabesques. Passing through the
forest of columns inlaid with porphyry and purple crystals,
he came to the great courtyard which was filled with orange
trees and tropical plants. He was often found in the Great
Synagogue of ibn Shaprut in the company of his father. Of
all the synagogues in Cordova this was the most resplendent.
The entrance was formed by three arches. The ceiling and
floor were inlaid with many colored stones. Marble pillars,
holding oil lamps of bronze, supported the balconies. The
reading desk was decorated with red and gold cloth. The ark
was enclosed behind heavy bronze doors and was approached
by marble steps.

Moses was equally sensitive to the intellectual heritage
that was his in this "Athens of the West." To be born in the
city of Seneca and Averroës in the Golden Age of Moorish
Spain was a token of great promise. Many learned men lived
in Cordova at this time: physicians, philosophers, historians,
astronomers, and mathematicians. Trade in perfumes, shoes,
saddles, leather goods, and parchment still flourished; there
were hides from Saragossa, steel swords from Toledo, silks
from Valencia, and pottery from Calatayud. Oriental mer-
chandise came by way of the nearby port of Almeria. Cordova stood at the crossroads of the East and West.

Maimonides had the advantage of an illustrious family
background. His ancestry could be traced to the renowned
editor of the Mishnah, Rabbi Judah Hanasi. His father,
Joseph, was a scholar in his own right, trained in the Academy of the Talmudic authority, Joseph ben Migash. He was
a member of the Rabbinical Council and served as *dayyan*
or judge in Cordova, a position having been held by the head

of the family for several generations. He was known also for his writing in astronomy and mathematics as well as his commentaries on the Talmud and expositions of the Bible. But background and environment were not the only tutors of the boy in Cordova. It was the father's teaching and example that prepared Moses for his future position as the spiritual leader of Judaism. He taught the boy mathematics, science, and philosophy and instilled in him a profound respect for the Jewish faith. It is to be inferred from a letter of Maimonides to Samuel ibn Tibbon that the boy also studied under Rabbi Joseph ben Zadik, a colleague of his father. Moses was a precocious lad, delving into the problems of philosophy at an age when other boys were learning how to spell. As a man of some means, Maimon was able to give the boy many advantages otherwise impossible. The family lived in the residential section on the "marble street" which lined the bank of the Guadalquivir. Moses' days were spent studying the valuable manuscripts that were in his father's collection, receiving instruction from Maimon, and teaching his younger brother David the Haggadah and Hebrew grammar. Occasionally he and David loitered at the marketplace and the square where they saw Hebrew slaves redeemed. But Moses had no time for play or exercise and gave little thought to his physical well-being.

Few details are known of Maimonides' boyhood, but we can be certain that he acquired a liberal education in the philosophy of the Greeks, the astronomy of the Arabs, and the religious literature of the Jews. He found early in life the secret of the educated mind which is to see things in relation to each other and not as independent entities, to see everything in a cause-and-effect relationship, to see life whole.

This was the earmark of his mental outlook; he acquired perspective and balance and held in perfect equilibrium faith and reason, mysticism and ethics. These were the qualities that enabled him to become the guide of his people. He also had a premonition or consciousness of his destiny which gave him a sense of mission.

Puritan Revolt

The congenial situation in Cordova was not to last. Events occurred that were fraught with grave consequences, that transformed the peaceful, studious life of the boy into one of wandering in exile. A reaction to the enlightened rule of the Almoravids had sprung up in North Africa and now spread into Spain. The fanatical Almohades (or Puritans, as the followers were called) were rabidly opposed to the liberal tendencies of the time and called for a purer monotheism. The founder of the sect was Abdallah ibn Tumart, a man of religious zeal and political ambition. His *Confession* was an uncompromising expression of the unity, universality, and abstractness of God. His successor Abd el-Mumin overcame the Almoravids in Morocco and, invading Andalusia, captured Cordova in 1148. The invaders destroyed synagogues and churches. Jews and Christians alike were given the choice of apostasy or death. Abd el-Mumin later softened his policy of persecution by allowing the Jews to emigrate and many took advantage of the opportunity. Others suffered martyrdom or adopted for the time a semblance of the Moslem religion. They attended the mosque, as was required, but in the privacy of their homes prayed to the God of their fathers and followed the Talmudic laws. Such action seemed reasonable enough since both religions were alike monotheistic and had a common source in the Bible. Still others, while not accepting the Moslem religion, wore Moslem clothes and spoke Arabic in order to escape detection but were loyal to the Jewish religion.

It is possible that the Maimon family followed the latter course. At any rate, they were able to maintain their residence in Cordova for a few years, during which time Moses the student became the writer and scholar. At the age of twenty-three he wrote some commentaries on the Talmud, an essay on the Jewish calendar, and a short book on logic. In this last treatise, which he called "a modest contribution to the terminology of Logic," he maintained that anyone who hopes to acquire a good education should include this discipline in his curriculum. "Logic," he continues, "is not an isolated study that may be pursued for its own sake, but rather an indispensable instrument for the attainment of all other knowledge. . . . For logic is to reason what grammar is to language; the one lends precision to speech and the other gives precision to thought." Already his graphic transparent style was evident, and it was clear that Moses ben Maimon in his early twenties was already a gifted writer. The book on Logic was written in Arabic and was translated later into Hebrew by Moses ben Tibbon and still later into Latin by Sebastian Muenster. During this period the young scholar began what was to be known as the first of his great trilogy, the *Siraj* or Commentary on the Mishnah.

From 1150 to 1160 the Maimon family was driven from one city to another as the Almohades intensified their persecution. They migrated first to Almeria on the southern coast of Spain but were soon forced to move on. For the following eight years their movements are unknown. Finally, in 1160, Joseph, Maimonides' father, decided to leave Spain.

Fez

The family crossed the Mediterranean and settled in the Moroccan city of Fez. Here the father and David went into the jewelry business, while Moses pursued his studies and his writing. Why Fez was chosen as a supposed sanctuary from the Puritan persecution remains a mystery. It was here that Abdallah ibn Tumart had inaugurated his fanatical movement ten years before. Meanwhile he had subdued all the Barbary states and all non-Moslems were compelled to accept Islam or be killed. The city of Fez had become a hotbed of violence and intolerance. It was the last place on earth the Maimons would be expected to select for a home. There were some Christian communities in Europe which might have extended hospitality. On the other hand, the father probably thought that it was too late for him to try to adjust himself to the customs and language of a strange culture.

It has been assumed by many scholars on the basis of a later testimony of an Arab in Cairo that Maimon and his family adopted the Moslem religion in Fez. Others flatly reject this idea, arguing that Moses' opponents never accused him of apostasy—an accusation which would have been made by them if they had heard of his defection. The truth probably lies halfway between the two extremes. It did not strike either father or son as a sin or mark of infidelity to take a position of accommodation. Although they were never converted to Islam, they passed themselves off as Arabs and mingled with Moslem scholars. Privately they continued faithful to Judaism. This dual course of conduct was in no way different from their life in Cordova. It was, in fact, the contact with Moslem learning that had helped to make possible this great period of Jewish enlightenment. As to the ethics of the matter, they felt as Galileo later did, that it is better to live and contribute something to the world than stubbornly die as a martyr. This was not the first time that Jews disguised themselves in order to avoid death. We are told that many Jews during the Crusades wore a cross and otherwise disguised themselves as Christians in order to escape the sword.

A further reason for living in Fez, suggested by Solomon Zeitlin, was that only there could Moses find suitable sources for the continuance of his research and contact with other scholars.[1] It is true that he benefited greatly in his Talmudic studies through his collaboration with Judah ha-Kohen ben Shoshan, head of the Jewish community in Fez. He also profited by his association with Moslem scholars in the field of medicine. Although ibn Tumart boasted that "there is no church or synagogue in our land," he apparently had not interfered with secular education. On the contrary, the Almohavids encouraged the study of science and philosophy.

The policy of ostensible conformity to Islam while privately holding to the Hebrew faith was not without its dangers for the common people. Some of the Jews in Fez, compelled to give lip service to Islam by attending services at the mosque, were almost convinced that the Moslem religion was destined to replace Judaism and Mohammed to supplant Moses. Not a few were on the point of forsaking the Jewish religion. As a means of combating this tendency, Joseph wrote a *Letter of Consolation*. In this letter he reassured the wavering brethren that God had not deserted Israel. "We must no more doubt God's promises than we doubt His existence." His promises are of "eternal and irresistible validity." A wholehearted allegiance to the Law is the desirable way

[1] Solomon Zeitlin, *Maimonides* (New York, Bloch Publishing Company, 1955), pp. 7, 8.

but "he whose grip on it is only with the tips of his fingers has more hope than he who lets go of it altogether." Moses is still the messenger of God and his Law is still the perfect guide and must be followed. "Let us cling to our holy teachings as steadfastly as a drowning person clings to a rope that is thrown out to save him. Let us treasure the daily prayers that we have inherited from our forefathers."

Letter Concerning Apostasy

A Jewish resident of Fez wrote to a foreign rabbi for an opinion regarding those Jews who, in order to escape persecution, repeated the Moslem confession of faith, "There is no God but Allah, and Mohammed is his prophet." The reply was that such Jews were apostates and regardless of secret prayers they could not be called Jews any longer but only idol-worshipers and renegades. In the face of this ultimatum many considered giving up the Jewish religion completely. The only true course, the rabbi concluded, was to accept martyrdom; a Jew must hold religion more precious than life; to appear in the mosque was a blasphemy against God.

This advice was widely circulated and aroused feelings of utter dismay and guilt among the Anusim, as the quasi-apostates were called. It also aroused the resentment of Maimonides, who proceeded to write his own epistle. He could only regard the charge as applying to himself, since he also had been guilty of this "pretended" submission to Islam. Maimonides' *Letter Concerning Apostasy* was a vehement defense of the Anusim. Quoting the Talmud, he showed that it was not considered a sin for anyone to disguise himself in order to avoid being put to death. The great Rabbi Meir in the second century had done the same and no one ever questioned his orthodoxy. He cited the case of King Ahab who had betrayed God by worshiping idols but had later repented and was forgiven. The argument of Maimonides that there was a difference between the apostasy of *speech* and that of *action*—that merely to utter the Moslem formula is not so serious a transgression as an overt act—appears somewhat casuistical. He refers to a former instance where Jews were forced to take action contrary to the Law as compared with this situation in which it was only a matter of repeating the Islamic confession. He also distinguishes between the acceptance of idolatry "through no compulsion" but through one's own willful choice as over against a compelled outward conformity. Whoever is guilty of the former course, he writes, is an apostate, but whoever follows the latter, concealing his true identity, is still a Jew. "The present differs from previous experiences. In former cases Israelites have been called upon to transgress the Law in *action*. Now we are not asked to render active homage to heathenism, but only to *recite* an empty formula which the Moslems themselves know we utter insincerely in order to circumvent a bigot." He concludes: "If a man asks me: 'Shall I be slain or utter the formula of Islam?' I answer: 'Utter the formula and live.'"

This letter of reassurance undoubtedly kept many from forsaking Judaism altogether. Maimonides said that those who had profaned the Law should be treated with understanding and kindness, but his final advice was that the Jews should leave the country and seek a place where they could worship God in peace and not be coerced in anything. Only thus could they live in good conscience. He condemned the action of those who had determined to continue in their dual allegiance until the Messiah would come and lead them to the Holy Land. Such a course only intensified their transgression. No one could possibly know where or when a Messiah would appear. Those who for one reason or another could not leave the country, he concludes, should remain and seek to observe the Law in the privacy of their homes.[2]

The *Letter Concerning Apostasy*, written in Arabic when Maimonides was about twenty-seven years of age, thrust him into prominence as a leader and religious authority. He put his advice into action by going about the country consoling, teaching, and restoring the quasi-Moslems to their Jewish faith. But the resulting aggressiveness on the part of Moroccan Jews brought Maimonides into grave danger. Previously, just as in Spain, he had associated with Arab scholars and physicians and was generally presumed to be a Moslem, but now the Almohades, aware of his activities among the Jews, instituted an Inquisition aimed at those who relapsed from Islam. When some of the leading Jews of Fez were put to death, it became clear that Maimonides seemed destined to meet the same end. From this fate he was saved through the good offices of his friend, the Arab scholar, Abul Arab ibn Moisha. Many Jews suffered martyrdom, including Moses' teacher, Rabbi Judah ha-Kohen, who was burned at the stake.

Palestine

The Maimons now realized that their only remaining course was to leave the country. On the night of April 18, 1165, the family secretly boarded a ship for Palestine. Moses was at this

[2] Jewish authorities have always been divided on Maimonides' status in Fez. Graetz and Munk state that he was a pseudoconvert to Islam. Margoliouth, Yellin, and I. Abrahams hold that although Maimonides was casuistical in justifying the actions of those who openly professed the Moslem faith and privately adhered to the Torah, it does not follow that he himself took that course or became part Moslem. If he did, he probably saw no great sin in this form of electicism. Going to the mosque, studying with Arab scientists, and uttering Moslem prayers in his mind did not constitute apostasy.

time thirty years old. On the sixth day of the passage a violent storm arose, threatening to capsize the ship. "The sea was in a fury," Maimonides wrote, "and we were in danger of perishing." But the storm passed, and after a voyage of a month they arrived at Acre where, as he wrote, they "found a refuge from two evils—the storm of persecution and the dangers of the sea." The Maimons dedicated the day as a festival to be celebrated annually. They received a warm reception by the Jewish colony. Maimonides became a close friend of Japhet ben Elijah, the *dayyan*, and life once more took on a more favorable complexion.

After several months in which Maimonides continued his Talmudic studies, he decided to go to Jerusalem, partly to see the Holy City and partly to do penance for his Moroccan days. The family was accompanied by Japhet. They remained in Jerusalem three days, praying at the Wailing Wall and exploring sacred sites. Then they made a pilgrimage to Hebron, where Maimonides descended into the cave of Machpela and dedicated himself to the memory of the three patriarchs, Abraham, Isaac, and Jacob. He prayed: "Give me strength, O Lord, to fulfill my vows, and grant that I and all Israel may see a new and beautiful Holy Land rise out of the ruins upon which I now offer this prayer."

Happy as his sojourn in Palestine had been, Maimonides decided it was not the right place for him. The Jewish population, small and scattered, was destitute. There was no such cultural activity here as in Spain or Morocco. The First and Second Crusades had devastated the land and most of the Jews had been killed or exiled. The country offered no prospects either for the business of making a living or for Moses' writing. The family returned to Acre and toward the end of the year 1165 sailed to Egypt.

Alexandria

The Maimons disembarked at Alexandria where there were about 3,000 Jewish families in this ancient center of the Diaspora. The Jewish population in Egypt at the time was fairly large. The Jews were granted a considerable degree of autonomy under their own *Nagid* (Prince) and practically equal status with Moslems. The *Nagid* was the Jewish representative in the Egyptian government and exercised complete authority in both religious and secular matters, with power to appoint rabbis, synagogue officials, and judges. The office of *Nagid* had originated in the tenth century when the daughter of the Caliph of Bagdad, having married the king of Egypt, came to Cairo and inquired about the government of the Jews. When told that they had no secular ruler, she suggested to the king that he appoint a prince after the manner of the Babylonian government. A letter was written to the king of Babylonia, who responded by sending a prominent Jewish leader to Cairo and he was appointed *Nagid* over all Jews in Egypt.[3]

A few years before Maimonides' arrival in Egypt the *Nagid* Samuel had died. He had been deposed and imprisoned through the machinations of Yahya-Zuta, who claimed that Samuel was a traitor to the Egyptian government. After a chaotic interim, Zuta obtained the position and was in office later when the Maimons moved to Fostat, a suburb of Cairo. He did not enjoy the confidence of the Jews; in fact, he was universally opposed because of his intrigue against Samuel.

If political conditions were in a state of confusion, the

[3] See Jacob Mann, *The Jews in Egypt and in Palestine under the Fatimid Caliphs* (London, Oxford University Press, 1920–22), Vol. I, pp. 251–252.

religious and intellectual climate of Egyptian Jewry was in a much worse condition. This surely was no Spain. There were no learned rabbis, no great poets, no philosophers of repute. Furthermore, the spiritual life was at a pathetically low ebb with little zeal for the Law. The Karaites had become highly influential even in political circles. Such a situation was ruinous to the Rabbinical movement and became an immediate concern of Maimonides. As we have previously indicated, Karaism, in its emphasis on the Scripture rather than tradition, must be credited with helping to develop biblical exegesis and philology; but its reactionary character proved a hindrance to the growth of Judaism. Maimonides' first act in Alexandria was to combat the influence of this group. In this enterprise he was successful, not in trying to destroy the sect, but in seeking to conciliate the adherents and restore them to the traditional faith. By treating them as friends, he was able to modify some of the Karaite practices and lessen their influence and also strengthen the Rabbinical forces.

While Maimonides was still in Alexandria, his father died and his brother David was drowned in the Indian Ocean. This double tragedy left a permanent mark on Moses.[4] David and the father had established a good business but now with their death the source of income was lost. Maimonides later wrote of this disastrous period and of his brother: "For a full year I lay on my couch, stricken with fever and despair. Many years have now gone over me; yet still I mourn. He grew up on my knees; he was my brother, my pupil. He went abroad to trade that I might remain at home and continue my studies. My one joy was to see him."

[4] According to some authorities David died in 1174 after Maimonides had moved to Fostat.

It was at this time that Maimonides, in order to support himself and his brother's widow and daughter, started to practice medicine. His work in this capacity, however, was limited and was subordinated to his one consuming desire, which was to finish the *Commentary on the Mishnah*.

CHAPTER THREE

The Good Life

The Doctrine of the Mean

IN 1168 Maimonides completed his *Commentary on the Mishnah*, which he had begun ten years before. Biographers differ on the question of his residence at this time, some holding that he had moved to Fostat and others that he lived in Alexandria until 1171. He was now thirty-three years of age. The work had been accomplished in the face of religious persecution, personal suffering, and constant moving about. "This is the work of an exile," he writes, "a man whom God has sent wandering from one end of the earth to the other. Some of these pages have been written on land and some on the sea."

He called the book *Siraj*, the Arabic word for Light, an appropriate title, for it was indeed an illumination for the bewildered Jews lost in the confusing and complicated labyrinths of the Mishnah. Life in the Diaspora had always been a precarious one. In the Moslem world, voluntary or involuntary heresy, intermarriage, and lack of learning had resulted in a gross neglect of the Torah and an ignorance of the Talmud, which was a heterogeneous mass of unintelligible material in which the passing and the permanent, spiritual truth and casuistical trivia, were scarcely to be distinguished. It was Maimonides' task to sift, clarify, and simplify this body of legal precedent for the common people.

The *Siraj* was written in Arabic, the vernacular of Jews in the Moslem countries, but later it was translated into Hebrew, some of it in Maimonides' lifetime. He succeeded well in bringing order out of chaos, in giving meaning to Talmudic laws, and, what is more important, in defining the Good Life for all persons. In this last he continues the work of his predecessors in Spain in fashioning a philosophy of life based on the union of Greek rationalism and Hebrew ethics. In such a combination of Hebraism and Hellenism, he proposes for the ideal life the Aristotelian doctrine of the Mean (μεσότης). "Nothing in excess" defines true virtue. The mature person is balanced, symmetrical. The extremities of excess and deficiency, intemperance and asceticism, are both evil. The Greek sense of harmony and beauty must be affixed to the austere Hebraic sense of moral duty. The Hellenic reverence for beauty must be supplemented by the prophetic demands of the moral law and righteousness. Beauty itself is inadequate for the ideal life. There must be a beauty or harmony that is seen in morality. The balanced person has humility without obsequiousness, self-assurance without conceit, benevolence without ostentation.

In his introduction to the *Commentary*, Maimonides defines the difference between the written word and oral tradition. He wisely acknowledges that Moses did not write the Law but interpreted it orally and generations later it was reproduced in written form.[1] Both written and oral tradition

---

[1] Elsewhere Maimonides seems to follow the traditional or noncritical view that the Law was delivered to Moses in its completeness, a divine revelation. Most biblical scholars from the middle of the nineteenth century on have accepted the Documentary or Development Theory of the Pentateuch, suggested in part by such scholars as Astruc, Eichhorn, deWette, Hüpfeld, and Kuenen and finally stated as a definite theory by Graf and Wellhausen; namely, that the first five books of the Bible represent a composite authorship, being made up of four distinct strands or traditions (J—850 B.C.E., E—750 B.C.E., D—621 B.C.E., and P—500 B.C.E.), and that no written material comes from the time of Moses.

are sacred as the word of God. The distinction between canonical and uncanonical writings as defined by the Council of Jamnia (90 C.E.) does not enter into his discussion. On the whole, therefore, it seems that Maimonides takes a fairly non-critical view of the Scripture as compared with Hivi, Saadya, ibn Janah, Rabbi Isaac of Toledo, and Abraham ibn Ezra.

As to the prophets, he shares the modern distinction between the *nebiim* as forthtellers and as foretellers. They were neither clairvoyants, predicting the future, nor miracle workers, appealing to the senses. They were inspired messengers of God with a body of truth that was its own witness within and had no need of external proof.

In the section entitled "Sayings of the Fathers," Maimonides supplements the proverbs of the ancients with his own wise comments. In "The Eight Chapters," an introduction to "The Sayings of the Fathers," he tempers the Jewish moral teaching with Aristotelian logic. He speaks of sin as disease and the moralist as a physician who has knowledge of the soul and the power to cure the disease. A person's mind or soul can be sick, not knowing the difference between evil and good. Such a diseased person should consult the moral teacher just as the physically sick person consults the medical expert. In this we find an anticipation of modern psychiatry.

The Future Life

Maimonides gives considerable space in the *Commentary* to the doctrine of the future life. In this area his contribution to religious philosophy is his substitution of a spiritual conception for the common materialistic view. He does not consider the denial of the possibility of another life but does go so far as to condemn the doctrine of rewards and punishments as the criterion for living the good life while on earth and concludes that "virtue is its own excuse for being." The mature person lives the good life not from fear of going to hell and the hope of going to heaven but because of the satisfaction of his own soul. He does not grudgingly live a pious life from a sense of duty in order to receive a pay envelope from God Almighty but because of his desire for growth of soul. The present life is not just a painful price to be paid for entrance into Paradise but a part of an eternal growth.

One's conception of the *Olam Haba,* or future world, depends on one's intelligence. The common view (Jewish, Moslem, and Christian) was that the righteous were given a ticket to Heaven, a city of eternal bliss where the streets were paved with gold, the rivers were filled with wine and oil, where the saints lived in mansions made of precious stones and spent their time eating and drinking. Conversely, Hell was a place of diabolical torture where the bodies of its victims were consumed by eternal fire. Maimonides describes other conceptions of the future life: a Messianic Age in which the chosen ones will live as kings, as a physical existence after the resurrection in which families will be united, and as a condition on earth where one creates his own heaven and hell.

The utilitarian view, complains Maimonides, was the result of a literal interpretation of Scripture in which preacher and people were alike guilty. The sages wrote in symbolic, figurative language and never intended that their words should be taken literally. The wise reader looks for the hidden meaning in the parable. To clarify this idea and also in criticism of the materialistic interpretation, he compares adults with school children who have to receive awards as an incentive to study. The pupil at first has no appreciation of the inherent values in study; consequently the teacher offers candy and toys as a reward for studiousness. Later, the nature of the compensation changes to clothes, money, or reputation. Likewise, the average person has to be bribed into goodness by the promise of heavenly rewards. He is incapable of following the Law for its own sake, of living the exemplary life for the glory of God and the inner satisfaction of self. The only true goodness is an uncalculating goodness, a piety that expects no reward.

Surprisingly, Maimonides concludes that a concession is necessary to the unlettered person who is unable to understand the spiritual view but must live on the basis of punishment and reward—a solution employed by the Catholic and, to a great extent, the Protestant church today. The mass of people must be encouraged in their religious life by the promise of future compensation and are told that they will be punished if they are unfaithful. This reasoning, however, was only a means to the end that gradually people would attain the more mature motive of love and goodwill for their own sake. Goodness, then, will be its own reward. "He who desires to serve God from love must not serve in order to win the future world; but he does the right and eschews the wrong because he is a man and owes it to his manhood to perfect himself; and this effort brings him to the type of perfect man, whose soul shall live in that state which befits it—in the world to come."

This is Maimonides' conclusion of the matter: Heaven or the life of blessedness exists in a person's soul to the extent that he earns the right to it. To the degree that a person moves toward the Light in the present world will he be in a position to appreciate the Divine in the next. Eternal living is more important than rewards of immortality, for the first is qualitative and the second is quantitative. Of immortality we can really know nothing for a certainty. "If we cannot define the exact nature of our life after death, it is because of the limitations of human language and the poverty of human thought." Surprisingly he bypassed the question of the bodily resurrection. In keeping with his nonmaterialistic view of Heaven, he would be expected to reject flatly the naïve belief in a physical resurrection, but his teaching on this point is ambiguous at best.

The Thirteen Articles

As part of the *Commentary* Maimonides drew up thirteen basic principles of Judaism which were to be binding on every Jew.

1. Belief in the existence of a Creator, the Cause of all life.

2. Belief in the unity of Deity.

3. Belief in the incorporeality of God, without attributes.

4. Belief that God is eternal, without beginning or end.

5. Belief that all worship and adoration are due Him alone.

6. Belief in prophecy.

7. Belief that Moses was the greatest of all prophets and will never be superseded.

8. Belief that the Law was given in its entirety by God to Moses on Sinai.

9. Belief in the immutability of the Law.

10. Belief that God knows the acts of man.

11. Belief in reward for the righteous and punishment for the wicked.

12. Belief in the coming of a Messiah.

13. Belief in the resurrection of the dead.

Some of these principles seem to run counter to statements appearing elsewhere in the writings of Maimonides. It seems inconceivable that with his presumed familiarity with the Torah, its contradictory recensions, its different styles of writing, and its references to post-Mosaic events, he could believe the "Law was given in its entirety by God to Moses on Sinai." The thirteen beliefs were not accepted without dissent, but they were nevertheless incorporated in the ritual of the synagogue. This set of beliefs, coming at a time when Judaism had no universally recognized authority, did much to hold the widely scattered Jews together, but Maimonides' accompanying statement—that whoever rejected any of these articles of belief was a "heretic and an unbeliever, and it is a duty to hate him and destroy him"—estranged many intellectuals. The anathema sounds too intolerant for the Rambam. Controversy raged and still does over the question of interpretation: are the items to be taken on face value or with mental reservations? It would seem that regardless of interpretation such dogmatic declarations do not represent the real Judaism any more than the Apostles' Creed, or the Nicene Creed, put together by ancient fanatics to counteract heresy, represent the true spirit of Christianity. Canons and creeds always appear in times of crisis. The Council of Jamnia, the Council of Nicea, the Council of Trent, the *Augsburg Confession*, the *Sixty-seven Articles*, *The Westminster Confession*, the *Institutes of the Christian Religion*—all these in turn may have brought solidarity to the respective groups in the face of heresy and doctrinal confusion, but they also produced bigotry and intolerance automatically, excluding from the fellowship all who did not accept their fine points of dogma. One can only take the charitable view that the Thirteen Articles of Maimonides do not really represent his view of Judaism, that he did not assume a strict conformity but a flexible interpretation. As they stand, they contain little that reflects the ethical genius of Israel.[2] Judaism always was, and still is, primarily a religion of deed, not creed.

It was in Europe rather than in Egypt that the *Commentary* was first recognized. Later it was universally accepted as a part of the Talmudic literature, and sections of it were translated into German and Spanish. The first complete Hebrew edition appeared in 1492.

[2] Belief in the future life and resurrection is not found in the Pentateuch but comes from postbiblical tradition. Crescas and Abraham ben David severely criticized the *Thirteen Principles* as unrepresentative of Judaism.

CHAPTER FOUR

Saladin the Magnanimous

End of a Dynasty

WE CAN BE FAIRLY CERTAIN that by 1171 Maimonides had moved from Alexandria to Fostat, a suburb of Cairo. The previous four years had been tumultuous ones in Egypt, Palestine, and Syria. In 1169 Saladin, the nephew of the Vizier of Damascus, having helped in the defense of Egypt against the King of Jerusalem, was appointed Vizier of Egypt by the Fatimid Caliph. As Vizier of all Egypt, Saladin determined to take Jerusalem, which, fourteen years later, he succeeded in doing. For several years after his appointment he faced serious domestic troubles. In religion he found himself between two fires, being the official representative of the Sunnite (orthodox) Sultan of Damascus and also the Vizier of the Shiite (heretical) Caliph of Egypt. He encountered opposition in the palace from the head eunuch, a Sudanese who hitherto had exercised much authority, as well as from the Caliph himself, who resented his increased power. The eunuch conspired with the King of Jerusalem in an attempt to oust Saladin, but the Vizier heard of the intrigue and had the eunuch arrested and put to death. This aroused the partisan Sudanese troops of the palace to mutiny, but they were promptly subdued. Even Nureddin, the Sultan of Damascus, feared the growing prestige of his lieutenant and planned an attack, but his death put an end to that plot.

Meanwhile, the Crusaders recognized that Egypt under Saladin, who was still a Syrian general, was a formidable threat to Palestine. The King of Jerusalem, aided by the Franks, attacked the port of Damietta but was driven off, and the King was compelled to sign a peace treaty with Egypt.

Saladin's military successes brought him into favor with both the Sunnites and the Shiites. His next act was to remove el-Adid, the ailing Caliph, from office. Now with Nureddin and el-Adid out of the way, the dangers of attack from without and revolt from within were eliminated. Saladin became Sultan of Egypt and inaugurated a regime of enlightenment which lasted a quarter of a century. Both he and Alfadhel, the Vizier whom he had appointed, were tolerant, genial, and fond of learning. All subjects were treated equally, and the Jews especially became prosperous and influential. Saladin beautified Cairo and rebuilt Fostat, which had been burned to the ground at the order of Shawar, the former Vizier of Egypt, so that it would be useless to the King of Jerusalem.

Saladin was not called the Magnanimous without reason. His recapture of Jerusalem in 1187 was not accompanied by the senseless massacre which had followed the entry of the Christians in 1097. Of the 300,000 Franks who started out with Godfrey of Bouillon only 20,000 survived to enter Jerusalem. After a three-week siege, these frenzied Christians, followers of the Prince of Peace, swept into the city and slaughtered all in sight. The Jews, who had fled to their synagogues for sanctuary, were burned to death as they prayed. The Moslems were beheaded wherever they were found. "They cut down with the sword everyone whom they found in Jerusalem," wrote the Archbishop of Tyre; "the victors were spattered with blood from head to foot." According to Raymond of Agiles, an eyewitness, "the blood of the massacred reached to the very knees and bridles of the horses." The carnage continued until sundown when the gory conquerors proceeded to the Church of the Sepulchre, "sobbing for excess of joy." They knelt in prayer and recited together: "This is the day which the Lord hath made. Let us rejoice and be glad in it."

No such butchery occurred when Saladin retook the city. The Christians were given their freedom and permitted to leave the city unmolested. Priests were allowed to remain and offer masses in Jerusalem, Nazareth, and Bethlehem. He later opened the city to the Jews, gave them complete autonomy, and permitted them to rebuild their synagogues and schools. As Vizier and Sultan of Egypt, Saladin respected the sincerity of all people who were of other faiths. Many incidents are related of his generous attitude toward the Jews and his defense of individuals who had been mistreated.

Letter to Yemen

Arriving in Fostat, Maimonides continued the practice of medicine which he supplemented by lecturing. There is reason to think that he also retained the jewelry business of his brother and went into partnership with ibn al-Moshat, a close friend. Fostat became a more cultural city under Saladin who established schools of higher learning and libraries and thus provided a more favorable atmosphere for Maimonides' research.

At this time (1174) the Rambam came into greater prominence in the Near East by reason of his letter to the Yemenite Jews. Yemen, known in antiquity as Arabia Felix and as the land of the Queen of Sheba, after being the object of a struggle between Christianity and Judaism, fell to Islam. The man in power, a Shiite Mahdi, was a religious fanatic who persecuted the Jews by offering them the choice of "Islam or death." Three thousand Jews capitulated and adopted the

Moslem faith. Others interpreted the times as the beginning of the Messianic Age and several false Messiahs arose to lead the people astray. One, an apostate Jew, announced that God had called him to destroy Judaism and establish Islam as the only true religion. Another claimed to be the forerunner of the real Messiah who would soon appear. He told the people to repent and prepare themselves for the coming Kingdom by giving their possessions to the poor. The country was swept with confusion, and those who kept a precarious hold on their faith were at a loss to know what to do.

It happened that at this time one of Maimonides' students, Solomon ha-Kohen, came to Yemen. He told the Jews about his great teacher and urged them to seek his help. Joseph al-Fayumi, the local leader, wrote to Maimonides describing the sad plight of the Yemenite Jews. Maimonides' reply, the *Letter to the South,* became one of the gems of medieval Jewish literature. It was written in Arabic but was later translated into Hebrew. Recognizing the situation as another Fez, he begged the Jews not to forsake their religion but to accept persecution as the price for the new age which was to come. The Jews have always been persecuted, he wrote, by the Babylonians, the Greeks, the Christians, and the Moslems. The subtlety of the last attack lay in the argument that the truth was revealed to Israel at Sinai but had been superseded by the greater truth of Islam. "But Israel cannot be destroyed," he continued; "it is your duty to strengthen each other and to raise your voice in a faithfulness which shall never fail and which shall make known publicly that God is a unity, unlike all other unities; that Moses is His prophet; that the Law from the first word to the last was spoken by the Creator to Moses; that nothing is to be abrogated in it, nothing to be changed, nothing to be added thereto nor taken

53

therefrom; and that no other Law than this will ever come from the Creator." Again we see the shortsightedness which polemic always creates, limiting the revelation of God to a certain time and a certain man. (Historic Christian dogma commits precisely the same offense in claiming for Jesus a cosmic status as "the Son of God" sent to earth to redeem all mankind.)

After this introductory admonition Maimonides proceeds to refute the claims of the false Messiahs and the apostates. He denies that the Bible prophesies the coming of Mohammed. Any mention of the coming Messiah would naturally refer to an Israelite. He could understand why some desperate Jews in their ignorance might be attracted to the impostors but he was surprised that their leaders could be tricked by such madmen. No one could know the time, place, or identity of the Messiah to come; but a Messiah will come, he predicted, and will appear in Palestine. Meanwhile, it was the part of wisdom to remain loyal to their religious heritage and not provoke the Moslem rulers to violence, for severe persecution would surely break out at the announcement of a Jewish Messiah who aspired to leadership.

The letter, which was read in all Jewish communities of Yemen, achieved its purpose of restoring unity and discipline in South Arabian Jewry. Maimonides realized the danger to the Yemenite Jews if his letter became known to Moslem authorities. There were plenty of apostates from Judaism who stood ready to use any such evidence to stir up a turmoil. One of the false Messiahs fell into the hands of the Moslems. When captured, he shouted: "I am a messenger of God and I am ready to prove it." "What is the proof?" he was asked. "Cut my head off and it will miraculously return to my shoulders and I shall come to life again," was the reply. The ruler accepted the challenge and decapitated the man; but the miracle of restoration failed to work!

In 1174 Saladin's brother became ruler of Yemen, and conditions for the Jews improved in every way. To this day the name of Maimonides is venerated in the prayers of the Yemenite Jews.

Spiritual Leader

The fame of Maimonides as counselor, adviser, scholar, judge, Talmudic authority, and physician spread far and wide. He was regarded both as the most learned man in Egypt and the spiritual leader of the Jews throughout the Moslem world. One of the ways in which his leadership found expression was through his correspondence, which now reached enormous proportions. Requests for legal and rabbinical advice came from many foreign countries. He tells us that he answered all these letters personally and refused to employ a secretary, a fact corroborated by the discovery in the Genizah in Cairo of several autographed letters. His replies, even in questions of legal procedure, were direct and uncasuistical. Many of his *Responsa* are valuable today as interpretation of Jewish law and theology. In dealing with religious matters he followed the Bible and Talmudic tradition, but at the same time he tried to interpret the teaching in the light of the changing needs and conditions of the day.

The questions addressed to Maimonides ran the gamut of ecclesiastical and social life. A correspondent in France was concerned about astrology. Did the constellations influence human destiny? Should a Jew study astrology? The Rambam replied that there are three kinds of truth. The first is that of sense perception; our eyes and ears give us empirical evidence. The second is that which has been established by science: principles or axioms that are mathematically verifiable. The third source of truth is that which has been handed down by the Prophets. To ascertain the validity of an idea one must subject it to these three tests. Astrology meets none of these tests. It is "sheer stupidity, nothing but fantasy," acceptable only to the uninformed. "There is not a particle of scientific evidence to support it. The only study about the stars that deserves the name of science is Astronomy. For Astronomy supplies us with the key to the mystery of the Heavens and the mind of God." Astrology, he continues, violates the doctrine of free will. If it were true that our actions were determined by the course of the stars, there would be no point in following the teachings of Moses or the prophets. Why try to follow the path of righteousness if we are fated by our stars to follow another path? Without human choice there can be no rationality or ethical living. "Our ancestors, relying upon the stars, refused to resort to arms; and therefore our First Temple was destroyed. This old superstition still persists among us. We call upon the stars to save us, not knowing that our safety lies within ourselves." If there are some isolated passages in the Talmud that favor astrology, he argued, we can only be guided by today's reason rather than yesterday's superstition.

In another letter Maimonides rebuked a Jewish scholar who had offended a convert from Islam by deprecating his background. "When thy teacher called Moslems idolators he sinned grievously. Let him fast and pray; perhaps he will find forgiveness. Even if he had been in the right and thou in error, it was his duty to be gentle. . . . How great is the duty which the Law imposes on us with regard to proselytes! In the case of strangers we are bidden to love with the whole force of our affection."

The *Responsa*, written over a period of years in Fostat, were the essence of brevity, clarity, and sympathetic understanding. His judgments were greatly influential in molding Jewish social and religious customs for centuries to come. He was truly a light unto Israel.

In 1176 Saladin returned to Egypt from Damascus, where he had subdued the Franks, and was proclaimed King of Syria. His first act was to remove the unpopular Zuta as *Nagid* and to transfer the office of Exilarch from Damascus to Cairo. Maimonides, now recognized as spiritual leader of the Jews in Egypt, worked with the Exilarch in issuing legal decisions. Under Saladin, the Sunnite religion, which followed tradition as well as the Koran, became the official form of Islam. Also through Maimonides' influence, the Karaites, opponents of Talmudic Judaism, were won over to the Rabbinic tradition. Maimonides pursued a conciliatory policy toward the Karaites and permitted the Jews to associate with them, but he was strictly opposed to Jews' adopting Karaite practices. "Conquer their stubbornness by your friendliness," he advised, "treat them not with hatred, but with respect. Eat their food and drink their wine. But do not yield to their errors and their heresies." This achievement alone, as Nahmanides says, was enough to assure the Rambam a foremost place in Jewish history.

Maimonides was equally friendly toward Moslems and Christians. He suggested exchanges of knowledge between Christians and Jews. He welcomed converts from Islam as worshipers of the same God and searchers of the same divine truth. Egyptian Jewry had departed far from the Rabbinical tradition and suffered not only from the nonconformity of the Karaites but was split into two factions. In old Cairo there were two synagogues: one followed the Babylonian schedule for the Sabbath, reading of the Torah in one year; the other used the Palestinian system of three years. There were other differences in ritualistic practices. Egyptian Judaism indeed was half Moslem in its customs.

As spiritual leader, Maimonides did much to correct this situation. He raised the people to a new mental and spiritual level, brought order into the synagogue service of worship, established new regulations aimed at the rejuvenation of the Jewish religion and a return to the Prophetic and Rabbinic tradition, and brought about a reconciliation of the contentious factions. He became, in the words of Abram Sachar, "the intellectual arbiter of the Jewish world." [1]

[1] Sachar, *op. cit.*, p. 180.

CHAPTER FIVE

The Torah's Golden Lessons

The Code of Maimonides

Brief his message—the quintessence
Of the Torah's golden lessons—
Give thy days to peaceful labor,
Serve thy God, and love thy neighbor.

THUS DID THE POET Jehuda Charisi epitomize Maimonides' *Mishneh Torah*, capturing the essential spirit of Judaism and the Rambam's interpretation of it. But brief it was not, for it comprises fourteen lengthy books and one thousand chapters. It was completed in 1180 after ten years of intensive labor.

The *Mishneh Torah*, like the Code of Hammurabi, was a compilation of existing laws; but it was something more than a mere codification. Maimonides added new laws which had no historic authority and even issued legal decisions contrary to the original Talmud. It was a rereading of the Law, an interpretation of the whole range of legal precedent from Moses to his own day. It was written in Mishnaic Hebrew rather than Arabic or classical Hebrew because in his mind it was more in keeping with the subject and more intelligible to the average reader.

The Code sets forth a decision on every question related to the ritualistic, religious, ethical, and social life of the Jews. The first book, *Sefer Ha-Mada* (Book of Religious Philosophy) deals with the fundamental principles of Judaism, the recognition and worship of God as Creator, and the necessity of knowing the Law.

It was Maimonides' aim in this epoch-making work to hold in perfect balance the ritualistic and the ethical emphases in Judaism. A superficial reading of these thousands of pages might leave the reader wondering where the prophetic element appears as he encounters endless differentiations in the interpretation of juridical provisions. In Book Three, on the *Seasons*, for instance, there are 649 laws indicating what is permitted and what is not permitted on the Sabbath, most of them meticulously hairsplitting, and yet there is the saving stipulation that "the commandment of the Sabbath, like all other commandments, may be set aside if human life is in danger, for the mere possibility of danger to human life overrules the Sabbath; it is forbidden to delay such violation of the Sabbath for the sake of a person who is dangerously ill, for the Scripture says: 'Which if a man do, he shall live by them' (Lev. 18:5), that is to say, he shall not die by them." [1] True, the Code omitted none of the trivial details of the Talmud, but it not only systematized them but related them to the spiritual principles of Judaism. Maimonides never forgot that ethical fruits flower only from spiritual roots. Scriptural and Rabbinical precepts are guides but they must be grounded in "wisdom and faith."

The Code was not without its defects, as contemporary and later critics pointed out. Unlike former Talmudic redactors who usually documented all opinions, naming the authorities involved, Maimonides omitted all mention of the Tannaim and Amoraim whose views were embodied in the Talmud itself. In the inclusion of new *Halakot*, or legal decisions, in addition to and sometimes contrary to the Gemara,

[1] See *The Code of Maimonides, Book Three: The Book of Seasons*, translated and edited by Solomon Gandz and Hymen Klein (New Haven, Yale University Press, 1961), p. 11.

Maimonides, it was claimed, failed to distinguish between principles of permanent validity and deductions that were only applicable to passing situations. His own opinions were stated categorically without reference to any authority. It was possible to infer from his Introduction that the work superseded all previous redactions and actually rendered the Talmud obsolete and unnecessary. He stated that the *Mishneh Torah* was "so complete that no other book will be necessary for the student of the Talmud; for a thorough understanding of Judaism one must have this book." There can be no doubt that Maimonides was too dogmatic in his decisions, but that he meant to supplant the Talmud with this book is questionable. It is hardly likely that he could be guilty of such presumption. The title itself suggests that the book is secondary to the Torah (*Mishneh:* second), a companion volume. He refers to the Talmud repeatedly and advises the reader to consult the Gemara particularly. Regarding his failure to mention names in the Tannaim and other sources, he insisted that his one purpose was to simplify the *Mishnah* for the layman and not confuse him by detailed notes and references. Between the two dangers of dogmatism and confusion he chose the former. It must be added however that he did list all previous compilers of the *Mishnah* in his Introduction.[2]

In the *Mishneh Torah* legal precepts are interfused with

[2] The expansion of the Torah in the Mishnah was a long and continuous process, extended and interpreted by the Tannaim in the first two centuries, the Academies of the Amoraim in Palestine and Babylonia (200–250), and the Geonim of Babylonia (600–1030). Maimonides' sources were the final redaction of the Mishnah by Rabbi Judah (200), the Babylonian and Palestinian editions of the Talmud, the Midrashim and Targums, the Tannaitic and Gaonic literature, the codification of Saadya (ninth century), the decisions of Rabbi Joseph Migash (twelfth century) and the *Halakot* of Alfasi (twelfth century).

ethical values; letter and spirit are interdependent; love and duty inseparable. Reverence for God is meaningless without service to man. As in all his other writings, Maimonides' ethical and philosophical system is based on the rationalism of Hellenism and the justice of Judaism. He advocates the Aristotelian life of temperance and self-control, the life of physical as well as mental harmony. The concept of "nothing to excess" applies to the mind as well as to the body: in other words, fanaticism and drunkenness are equally evil. The mind must be nourished with "divine thought" and the body with "temperate food."

The *Mishneh Torah* begins with a statement of the existence of God, His unity and incorporeality, and man's duty of loving and serving God through prayer and the moral life. "The foundation of foundations and the pillar of all wisdom is the recognition that an original Being exists, who called all creatures into existence; for the recognition of this is a positive command and is the great principle on which all things hang." Then follows the codification of the laws through which the life in God can be achieved. At the end—reminiscent of the seer Isaiah—Maimonides looks toward the coming of the Messianic Age when "the earth will be filled with the knowledge of God as the waters cover the sea."

Praise and Censure

The *Mishneh Torah* was enthusiastically received throughout the Near East and Europe. Rabbinical scholars praised its technical perfection, and laymen expressed appreciation that they were now able to comprehend the laws of the Talmud and the principles of their own religion. Professional scribes everywhere began to make copies and poets lauded him in verse. Among the most loyal followers of Maimonides were his two students Solomon ha-Kohen and Joseph ben Judah ibn Aknin, whose admiration knew no bounds when the *Mishneh Torah* appeared. Ibn Aknin had been a forced "convert" to Islam but remained a faithful Jew and was well versed in Jewish law. At the age of thirty he moved to Cairo to be near his teacher. The mutual friendship matured through the years and lasted until the Rambam's death. Maimonides treated the young man as a son and remarked: "If I had none but thee in the world, my world would be full." It was for ibn Aknin that his greatest work, *The Guide for the Perplexed*, was written.

Opposition to the *Mishneh Torah* seemed almost to outweigh the commendation as the independent and liberal attitude of the author aroused heated controversy in many quarters. The immediate surge of adverse criticism came from the fear that Maimonides had set himself up as a Jewish pope and from the feeling that if this work became the one permanent authority, it would freeze the religion of Judaism into a static code of law and obviate all growth. This fear was in part justified, but although the *Mishneh Torah* did become the most authoritative guide, it did not prevent further amplification and diverse application of Talmudic law. Some critics accused Maimonides of pretended infallibility and censured him severely both for omitting reference to previous redactors and for supplanting the Talmud with his own work. This criticism also was not without some justification, at least in Yemen where the Talmud was almost forgotten. The Rambam received the stricture calmly and replied that he intended the book to be examined critically and compared with former recensions, and that it was not meant to supersede the Talmud. In many self-governing Jewish communities, the laymen, in their study of the Code, became so conversant with practical law that lawyers and Talmudists were almost rendered unnecessary.

Opposition from Abraham ben David of Pasquières in France was based on the unorthodox theology of Maimonides and his omission of sources. Because ben David was a recognized scholar his opinions were taken seriously, and many of his comments were included in later editions of the Code along with counter-remarks by Joseph Karo. Less scholarly but more vehement attacks were made by Samuel ben Ali, head of the Yeshiva at Bagdad. His reasoning was that the College of Bagdad was the original seat of Talmudic learning and since Maimonides had never attended it he could not pose as an authority on the Talmud. The Rambam had always been scornful of the luxurious life of the Bagdad College and the profligacy of its head. Consequently, the Gaon accepted the challenge with alacrity. Samuel's criticism was based not only on the danger of losing the primacy of Bagdad but also on theological grounds. As a superstitious person and a believer in astrology, he stoutly opposed Maimonides' rationalism and denial of miracles. Furthermore, the book had been written without any mention of or consultation with the Bagdad authorities.

It happened that Maimonides' friend Joseph ibn Aknin was in Bagdad during the controversy and took up the cudgels in defense of his master. The unrelenting attempts of Samuel ben Ali to discredit Maimonides had led some of the Rambam's followers to doubt his authority. Others, influenced by his spiritual interpretation of the future life, inferred that official Jewish teaching denied the doctrine of bodily resurrection. Some students in Damascus, meanwhile, had interpreted the *Mishneh Torah* as teaching only a spiritual resurrection. Maimonides' reply that a belief in the resurrection was an essential tenet of Judaism was ambiguous at best; whereupon Samuel seized the opportunity of quoting Hagadic and Midrashic teaching on the bodily resurrection, insisting on their literal meaning. He reinforced his case by referring to concurrent opinion in Moslem tradition. Ibn Aknin for a time fought alone against the Gaon but finally appealed to Maimonides for a defense of his own position. The Rambam refused to enter the fray, and in his letter to ibn Aknin he said he had foreseen this attack but could not bring himself to fight back. He was heartbroken that his young friend had suffered on his account and advised restraint and magnanimity rather than belligerence. "You will please me better by teaching positively what is true rather than by posing as my champion." He reminded ibn Aknin of the Gaon's concern in the matter and his natural resentment.

He has much at stake. He has to concern himself with what the multitude believes. Leave him to his trivialities; what does he know of the soul and of philosophy? Remember he is old and occupies a position of dignity, and you are young and owe his age and position respect. You ask me as to your plan of opening a school in Bagdad in which you will teach the Law with my Code as the textbook. I have already sanctioned your proposal. Yet I fear two things. You will be constantly embroiled with these men. Or, if you assume the duty of teaching, you will neglect your own business affairs. I counsel you to take nothing from them. Better in my eyes is a single *dirhem* gained by you as a weaver, a tailor, or a carpenter, than a whole revenue enjoyed under the auspices of the Head of Captivity.[3]

Maimonides' letter to ibn Aknin did not end the controversy. In response to inquiries from Yemenite Jews and others,

[3] David Yellin and Israel Abrahams, *Maimonides* (Philadelphia, Jewish Publication Society of America, 1936), pp. 144, 145.

he finally issued a statement on the doctrine of the resurrection. In it he refused to go beyond the statements he had made in the Code that the idea of the resurrection of the body defies natural law and that the final resurrection to *Olam Haba* would be that of the soul. He maintained that the whole question was controversial. It was clear that the Talmud and postbiblical tradition could be interpreted as favoring bodily resurrection, but his own view was that, since God was incorporeal, the future life would therefore be without a body and that it was crass ignorance and pure materialism to insist that the life in the hereafter was a physical existence.

Maimonides himself was later drawn into a controversy with Samuel ben Ali over the question of the office of Exilarch. With the death of the Babylonian Exilarch (c. 1190) Samuel opposed the appointment of the new candidate, in fact was against having an Exilarch at all. He regarded the office as superfluous in view of his position as Gaon. His view was that Diaspora Judaism was a religious community, not a political state, and therefore should be governed by a religious leader and scholar rather than a prince. Acting on this contention, Samuel ordained his favorite pupil Zekarya as the leading scholar and commissioned him to solicit funds in Aleppo for the Bagdad Yeshiva. Wherever Zekarya went he sang the praises of Samuel and belittled Maimonides. This brought him into conflict with ibn Aknin, who wrote to the Rambam about the matter. Again Maimonides took an aloof attitude, admonishing his pupil to ignore the dispute. He admitted that some of Zekarya's criticisms of the Code were valid. Ibn Aknin's opposition to Zekarya stemmed from the assumption that Samuel was the authoritative head of Babylonian Judaism and that he could collect contributions from Aleppo, which was in Saladin's jurisdiction.

It was Samuel's attempt to abolish the office of the Exilarch that aroused Maimonides. Rightly or wrongly, he claimed that the Exilarch represented a continuation of the ancient kings of Israel and had final authority over the Jewish community. The battle lines were clearly drawn. Samuel viewed Judaism from a cultural standpoint while Maimonides saw it as a national entity, a view which he shared with the poet Halevi and which vaguely foreshadowed the modern movement of Zionism.[4]

In spite of Samuel's objections, a new Exilarch was appointed in Bagdad. His first act was to seek the approval of Maimonides. The latter's endorsement, supported by all Egyptian Jews, was good evidence both of the Rambam's prestige and the high status of the position of Exilarch.

The controversy with ben Ali was a protracted one and later turned on the issue of Sabbath laws. The Gaon found a chink in Maimonides' armor in his reply to a friend in Bagdad concerning river travel on the Sabbath. Samuel pointed out that Sabbath laws were biblical and not Rabbinical as Maimonides claimed. The latter countered that those pertaining to travel on *water* were Rabbinical. The correspondence which followed is too casuistical to be rehearsed here. Maimonides emerged from these disputes with no appreciable loss of prestige in spite of his vulnerability at certain points and his condescending attitude toward his critics.

[4] Maimonides elsewhere asserts that the ruler of the Jewish community should be a scholar. The issue is still debatable. Historically speaking, it can be maintained that from 586 B.C.E. to the establishment of the modern state of Israel, "Jewry" and "Judaism" have been purely cultural or religious terms, nationality depending on the state in which a Jew happened to be born.

CHAPTER SIX

Medicine and Morality

The Sultan's Physician

DURING SALADIN'S REIGN (1169–1193) Cairo experienced a great cultural growth. He established the Collegiate Mosque, which provided courses of instruction in many subjects and housed the Fatimid library of 120,000 manuscripts. He built the citadel as a fortress for the city, later to become the seat of the magnificent Mohammed Ali mosque. Alfadhel, the former Fatimid Caliph, had continued to enjoy Saladin's confidence and was made Vizier. With Saladin abroad much of the time, Alfadhel from 1185 on was the virtual ruler of Egypt. He not only encouraged the arts and all branches of learning but was a scholar in his own right, "sovereign of the pen who threaded discourse with pearls of style." The Vizier regarded Maimonides as next to him in authority and heaped upon him many honors and responsibilities. Once when Alfadhel was on a mission in Mesopotamia, he wrote to the Rambam: "Bear me a message to the Nile; tell it that Euphrates can never quench my thirst." [1]

In 1184 Maimonides married the sister of Abul Maali, secretary to one of the wives of Saladin. At about the same time, Maali married Maimonides' sister; so the two men were closely related. We gather from a letter to ibn Aknin that Maimonides' first child, a girl, died at birth. In 1186 a son was born. Little is known of the Rambam's home life, but it is certain that he was devoted to his son and tutored him in the Talmud, mathematics, and other subjects.

[1] Yellin and Abrahams, *op. cit.,* p. 118.

In 1185 the Vizier made Maimonides his physician, a post which probably came through the influence of Maali and which the Rambam held for the succeeding thirty years. In this capacity he served not only the palace but the common folk. His fame in medicine even reached the ears of Richard the Lionhearted, who invited him to be his personal physician but Maimonides declined the honor. Medical authorities sought his advice, and the well-known Abd al-Latif of Bagdad traveled to Cairo to consult with him. The Arabian poet, Al-Said ibn Sina Almulk, paid him tribute in rapturous verse.

> Galen's art heals only the body,
> But Maimun's heals body and soul.
> If the moon herself were to submit to his art,
> He would deliver her of her spots,
> And he would save her from wasting away
> At the period of her decline.
> For evil and ignorance flee from his presence.
> When Maimun arrives, all suffering departs.

Maimonides' devotion to medicine is revealed in a letter to a friend: "Although from my boyhood the Torah was betrothed to me, and continues to hold my heart as the wife of my youth, in whose love I find a constant delight, strange women whom I first took into my house as her handmaids become rivals, and absorb a portion of my time." Chief among these mistresses was the practice of medicine.

Some historians have said that Maimonides studied medicine under Averroës, but this was disproved by S. Munk.[2] Maimonides mentions two Muslim physicians whom he consulted in Fez, and it is highly likely that he also gained much information from others. Be that as it may, we know that he

[2] See Munk's *Notice sur Joseph ben Ichouda* (*Journal asiatique*, XI, 1843), p. 31.

had studied Galen and Hippocrates in Arabic translations, the works of Al Rhazi, the Muslim medical authority, the *Canon Medicinae* of Avicenna, and the writings of the Egyptian physician, ibn Ridwan. Most of our information on Maimonides' medical activities comes through three Muslim authors of the thirteenth century: Abd al-Latif of Bagdad, ibn al-Qifti, and ibn Abi Usaybia. Also the Christian historian Barhebraeus (d. 1286) transcribed much of ibn al-Qifti's biographical material. Although there was no hospital in Cairo, Maimonides conducted classes or gave informal instruction to young students of medicine.[3]

As a Jewish doctor in a Moslem court, Maimonides encountered no little resentment and jealousy on the part of Arabian physicians. They frequently tried to embroil him in arguments so as to bring him into disfavor with the Sultan, but his wisdom and skill were too much for them. As for the Vizier, the religion of his physician had no bearing on his practice of medicine. There was, in fact, another Jewish physician in the employ of Saladin named Rabbi Nathaniel, a close friend of Maimonides and a man of rare ability. On one occasion, the story goes, a man was pronounced dead and was about to be buried when Rabbi Nathaniel recognized that the body was only in a state of catalepsy. He stopped the funeral and seemingly brought the man back to life. Nathaniel, it appears, accompanied the Sultan on military campaigns and foreign travel while Maimonides served as the resident physician.

In 1187 a former friend of the Rambam, a well-known

[3] Some of Maimonides' sources for medical knowledge were Al Rhazi (860–932), Avicenna (980–1036), Isaac Israeli (850–950?), Sabbato ben Abraham Donnolo (903–982?), Abu-al-Malid Merwan ibn Janah (11th century), Anvenzoar (12th century).

Moslem lawyer in Fez, visited Cairo. He had once been instrumental in saving Maimonides' life in an attack by some fanatics. In his later years, however, he had taken a hostile attitude toward his friend. Apparently in Fez he had thought Maimonides was a Moslem. Now that he found him ensconced in the Sultan's palace as a Jewish physician he became still more resentful. He informed the Moslem authorities that Maimonides was formerly a Moslem and was now an apostate to Judaism, an indiscretion punishable by death. The Vizier once more defended his physician by declaring that even if the Rambam had turned Moslem it was an involuntary or compulsory conversion which had no legality and from which apostasy was not considered a punishable offense.

The Jews of the Middle Ages had a noticeable predilection for medicine, a result of their contact with the Arabs, first in Babylonia and then in Spain. We are told that there were some fifty prominent Jewish scholars in twelfth-century Spain who were noted for their medical practice and writing.[4] For Maimonides medicine was a moral and religious necessity as well as a scientific discipline. Health and holiness were for him synonymous, a conviction which had Jewish roots, for the idea of ritualistic cleanliness went back to the time of Ezekiel. A sound body is a prerequisite for a sound mind: the good life and the healthy life are bound together. He was a strong advocate of "general condition" as a preventive of many ailments. Proper diet and simple, temperate living, he said, can be of great help in avoiding epidemics and various diseases. Thus in his mind good health became a moral as well as a physical question. It is not surprising therefore that

[4] Practically all the Jewish philosophers mentioned in Chapter One were known as much for their medical knowledge as for their philosophical and literary achievements.

his philosophical works are replete with medical observations and his medical research contains many ethical aphorisms. He set forth a few simple rules for the healthy life. One should eat to live, not live to eat, leaving the table when the appetite is not completely satisfied. Raw fruits should be eaten sparingly and unripe fruit avoided. The diet should be balanced; in summer one should eat cold foods and in winter, warm. Regular habits of evacuation should be maintained. The body requires eight hours of sleep daily. One should go to bed early but not immediately after eating. In order to insure good health one should engage in steady work. Sickness is caused by "too much eating and too little work. Out of every thousand deaths, one is due to the cruelty of nature; all the others are caused by the stupidity of man." For the maintenance of good health Maimonides prescribed walking, running, fencing, wrestling, ball playing, and deep breathing. He regarded athletics and games as only a means to health, not an end in themselves.

With Maimonides spiritual and physical health go hand in hand. Spirit and flesh grow weak or strong together. They cannot be dissociated. The ideal physician is a doctor of the soul as well as of the body. It is the responsibility of the physician to preserve the moral well-being of the patient as well as the physical, for only then could a harmonious and healthy society be nurtured.

Medieval Magic

Enlightened as Moorish Spain was, it must be remembered that it was still the Middle Ages. The common people were ignorant and Christians had no monopoly on magic and witchcraft. Even rabbis, at least the more fanatically religious, were inclined to be guided by the popular superstitions rather than scientific procedure. Many openly opposed Maimonides in his ministration to the sick on the grounds that health and sickness, good fortune and ill fortune, were in the hands of God and were not to be interfered with by man. The ancient belief that suffering is a direct result of sin, a punishment from God, as the friends of Job told him, still prevailed among even educated people.[5] If a man lived a virtuous life he would be rewarded with prosperity and good health; conversely, if he sinned he would experience adversity and suffering. The only relief for the afflicted was in prayer and penitence. The Talmud itself had warned against the use of medicine. If a physician tries to heal disease he is working against the will of God and is therefore guilty of a sin.

To this Maimonides replied that the Talmud also advised those who were sick to consult a doctor, that when settling in a new community to be sure "that it possesses three necessary things: a physician, a surgeon, and a bath-house." To refuse the help of a physician and rely only on God is just as foolish as refusing to eat in the belief that God will save one from hunger. The untrained doctor may well become the "devil's disciple," but the competent physician is a servant of God.

Another form of quackery or witchcraft was the custom of treating diseased people with amulets and incantations. This was the way of the Cabbalists and was simply a survival of the ancient biblical practice of exorcism. Sickness was still attributed to possession by an evil spirit, the remedy for which was to drive the devil out of the patient forcibly by flogging, burning, or otherwise inflicting punishment on the body.

[5] In the eighteenth century the clergy of France declared that the Lisbon earthquake, which killed 30,000 persons, was God's punishment of the people for their sins.

Maimonides declared war on superstition and sorcery. "Do not be deceived by this abracadabra," he wrote; "the holy names which they inscribe upon their charms have not the slightest power to cure disease. These quacks are nothing but self-deluded fools. They are probably sincere in their belief that their hocus-pocus possesses medical power. But a sincere madman is just as dangerous as one who is insincere." Many parents bought gold and silver charms or amulets for the protection of their children from disease. Maimonides declared that "a man who mumbled magic over a wound is no better than a sorcerer and that the 'healer' who spreads a prayer-shawl over a sick child is a sinner against man and a blasphemer of God." [6] Another custom in the Near East was that of feeding dog's liver to a person who had been bitten by a mad dog. Vehemently opposing such a practice, Maimonides declared that "neither science nor practical experience has ever demonstrated the efficacy of such a form of healing." Surprisingly enough, "sympathetic healing" and astrological theories regarding sickness were common among the Egyptian Arabs. Maimonides also openly opposed these ideas as unscientific and unproved.

Maimonides' medical writings were based largely on Galen; but in his practice he relied on experience and experiment. He recognized the fine line that exists between mind and body, the interaction of the mental and the physical, and the fact that some ailments which affect the body emanate from the mind and vice versa. In this observation there is an anticipation of modern psychological knowledge. A prefigurement of modern methods is also seen in his philosophy of preventive medicine. He repeatedly emphasized the impor-

[6] J. Münz, *Maimonides* (Boston, Winchell-Thomas Company, 1935), p. 181.

tance of proper diet, exercise, and personal hygiene in maintaining general health. If a person's general condition is good, he said, many diseases can be avoided. He prescribed drugs only as a last resort and only after it was clear that a controlled diet and proper living conditions were ineffective. There exist, he said, countless plants and herbs whose purpose is to supply food and medicine. This is not to say that he was a "nature" doctor. He had great faith in the salutary effects of a sound constitution and a positive mental attitude, but where the patient's disease was organic and beyond natural help he advised medical remedies.

Nothing to Excess

Maimonides' medical books were written between 1180 and 1200 in Arabic and were later translated into Hebrew and Latin. One of these, dedicated to Alfadhel, was a treatise on general health. In this volume he deals at length with diet, the avoidance of constipation and other stomach and intestinal disorders. He warns against overeating as the cause of many ailments. He advises (contrary to his own practice) daily exercise and fresh air. He recommends a periodic checkup and consultation with a physician. His suggested restrictions on sexual intercourse approached the ascetic: he warned against the dangers of coition indulged in by older people, by those subject to heart attack, by convalescents, by persons who are fatigued or intoxicated, and by all people before or after meals. In this connection he warned the Vizier against overindulgence and indicated ways in which he could avoid sexual desire. In the use of wine he follows his doctrine of the mean. Wine is highly beneficial in keeping one in good health as well as a remedy for illness. In moderation it is good especially for the aged. He continually warns against inordinate desire and advises moderation in all things. An intemperate craving for food, money, and pleasure leads to violence and social evils. The book closes with the sound advice that it is dangerous to change one's pattern of living—exercise, diet, work—suddenly. As one grows older, physical activity must be changed gradually.

In 1198 Saladin's son, Almalik, became Sultan and, upon ascending to the throne, made Maimonides his private physician. Two of the Rambam's medical writings were occasioned by the illness of the new Sultan. Almalik lived an epicurean life of overindulgence which resulted in a state of melancholia. When asked to treat the ruler, Maimonides wrote a set of rules which later took the form of a psychiatric treatise. In this work he pointed out the physical benefits of a wholesome mind and the adverse effects of a continued perversity of mind. In other words, he was saying that the worst evil is mental—the ungenerous, diabolical, and distorted mind, the mind that denies all goodness, calls white black and God the Devil. Evil thoughts, if persisted in, lead to evil deeds, even to disease and death. The life of self-control is the secret of good health. "A man who is captain of his own soul is a greater hero than the commander of hosts. Such a man will restrain himself in prosperity and will not lose himself in adversity."

Maimonides' book *Asthma*, the second treatise written for Almalik, who suffered from that ailment, was highly regarded at that time. Of more permanent value, however, was his book on *Poison and Its Cure*. This was written at the request of the Vizier as an aid in reducing the number of deaths caused by snakebites. Maimonides prescribed treatments and remedies for internal poisoning, bites from snakes and mad dogs, and for other cases of poisoning. For septic wounds, he advises bandaging tightly the limb just above the wound so as to stop circulation, sucking out the wound, treating it with alcohol, and keeping it open. For internal poisoning he recommends theriaca and mandrake. Dosage depends, he writes, on the severity of the poison, the general condition of the patient, and the nature of the poisoning or wound.[7] He warns against dressing wounds and advises letting the blood flow from them in order to carry away the poison. He prescribes a vegetable diet and strong wine. Much attention is given to the symptoms of poisoning and its remedies.

In all his medical writing Maimonides advocated preventive measures and the importance of general condition. His was the experimental method; where he had had no personal experience he refused to prescribe. Only those remedies which he had found to be effective and which had authoritative precedent were recommended. His practice encompassed every branch of medicine and he wrote treatises on each one. He even anticipated the modern books on sex in his *Physiology and Psychology of Married Life.*

Maimonides' *Aphorisms* (1190) was an encyclopedia of medical theory and practice, consisting of 1,500 maxims and precepts dealing with medicine, anatomy, physiology, pathology, symptomatology, diagnosis, etiology, therapeutics, gynecology, hygiene, physical education, and drugs.[8] It was, in his words, "a collection of the wise sayings of the Arabian

[7] The treatise on poisons, called by Maimonides "The Missive for al-Fadil," is extant in many excellent Arabic manuscripts and translations into Hebrew and Latin.

[8] Several Arabic manuscripts of the work are extant. The best, according to Max Meyerhof, is in the Gotha Library and is a copy of a copy made by Abul Maali Yusuf ibn Abdallah, Maimonides' nephew, who relates that he finished it in 1205. Another copy, in the Leyden Library, is from a Jewish scholar in Toledo (1324).

physicians, of Galen, and of the greatest of all physicians, Hippocrates"; but it was more than a compilation. He revised, simplified and interpreted the sayings of older authorities and in many instances added his own views. In other words, the book took on a philosophical complexion in the popular sense, emphasizing the interplay of mind and body, the importance of "thinking positively," the necessity of daily exercise, and the cultivation of spiritual values. In criticizing the philosophical outlook of Galen, he wrote:

> One of the commonest spiritual diseases is to prize your own religion and to despise all the others. He who suffers from this disease tries to belittle that which he does not understand. If he happens to be an authority in one field, his monomania leads him to believe that he can become an authority in every other field. One of the men who suffers pathetically from this spiritual sickness is the celebrated physician, Galen. In all his medical discussions he insists upon a logical and scientific point of view. The moment he enters the religious field, however, he leaves his logic and his science behind him. He becomes the fool trying to ape the Prophet. A doctor should stick to his drugs. Teach only that which you understand.[9]

It might be thought that Maimonides violated his own creed at this point, but it must be recalled that he was well trained in theology and philosophy. He was thoroughly familiar with previous writing in both fields.

Maimonides' last medical book was a lexicon or glossary of the names of drugs in several languages, a literary form well-known among Arab physicians in Spain and Morocco. He lists in alphabetical order some 2,000 drugs, generally giving first the Arabic name, followed by the Greek, Syriac, Persian, Berber, and Spanish forms. The fact that he included

[9] J. Münz, *op. cit.*, pp. 201, 202.

no Hebrew names confirms the belief that he wrote the Glossary for non-Jewish friends and pupils. In the introduction he writes as follows:

My aim in this book is to comment on the names of such drugs as exist in our time and are known to us and are in use in the Art of Medicine and met with in the medical books. I shall mention among the known simple drugs only those to which have been given more than one synonym (name), either in different languages, or by more than one in one and the same language. For one and the same remedy may have different names for people speaking one and the same language, either by a coincidence in the origin of the denomination or by a difference of the terminology with the inhabitants of different regions. I shall not mention, moreover, any very well known remedy to which the physicians do not give more than one name, Arabic or foreign. For the aim of this discourse is not to acquaint the reader with the different kinds of remedies by their description or the mention of their use, but the explanation of some of their names by other names. Likewise I shall not mention remedies which are well known and verified, such as, for instance, the fig, the grape, and the like, only on account of their Greek names, as they are mentioned in the books which came down to us and whose authors discussed and explained the matter. I make an exception where that Greek name preponderates among a great number of synonyms for the drug in question. I shall not mention, moreover, any remedy which bears rare and unknown names and which is not particularly useful in medicine.[10]

Other medical works were: *A Commentary on Hippocrates, The Causes of Disease*, and *An Epitome of Medicine.* The

---

[10] See *Essays on Maimonides*, Solo W. Baron, ed. (New York, Columbia University Press, 1941), pp. 293, 294. The Glossary is mentioned by ibn Abi Usaybia in his *Sources of Information on the Classes of Physicians*. It has been found in the Aya Sophia Library in Istanbul.

last is a succinct summary of Galen's sixteen volumes of medical knowledge, to which Maimonides added a history of medicine from the time of Galen to the twelfth century.

A letter to his friend Samuel ibn Tibbon gives us an intimate glimpse into his strenuous life as physician and spiritual leader.

I live in Fostat and the Sultan resides at Cairo. My duties to the Sultan are very heavy. I am obliged to visit him every day, early in the morning, and when he or any of his children or any of the inmates of his Harem, are indisposed, I dare not leave Cairo, but must stay during the greater part of the day in the palace. It also frequently happens that one or two of the royal officers fall sick, and I must attend to their healing.

When I return to Fostat in the afternoon I am almost dying with hunger. I find the ante-chambers filled with people, both Jews and Gentiles, nobles and common people, judges and bailiffs, friends and foes—a mixed multitude, who await my return. I dismount, wash my hands, go forth to my patients, and entreat them to bear with me while I partake of some slight refreshments, the only meal I take in the twenty-four hours. Then I attend to my patients, and write prescriptions and directions for their several ailments. Patients go in and out until nightfall, and sometimes even, I solemnly assure you, until two or more hours in the night. I converse with and prescribe for them while lying down from sheer fatigue, and when night falls I am so exhausted that I can scarcely speak.

In consequence of this, no Israelite can have any private interview with me except on the Sabbath. On that day most of the congregation come to me after the morning service, when I advise them as to their proceedings during the whole week; we study together until noon when they depart. Some of them return and read with me after the afternoon service until evening prayers. In this manner I spend the day.[11]

[11] See H. Adler, *Miscellany of Hebrew Literature.*

A Physician's Prayer

Maimonides' personal ethics is most profoundly expressed in his *Physician's Prayer*, a statement equaled only by the Hippocratic Oath for its integrity and humility.

O God, Thou has formed the body of man with infinite goodness; Thou hast united in him innumerable forces incessantly at work like so many instruments, so as to preserve in its entirety this beautiful house containing his immortal soul; and these forces act with all the order, concord and harmony imaginable. But if weakness or violent passion should disturb this harmony, these forces would act against one another and the body return to the dust whence it came. Thou sendest them to man Thy messengers, the diseases which announce the approach of danger, and bid him prepare to overcome them. The Eternal Providence has appointed me to watch o'er the life and health of Thy creatures. May the love of my art actuate me at all times; may neither avarice, nor miserliness, nor the thirst for glory or a great reputation engage my mind; for, enemies of truth and philanthropy, they could easily deceive me and make me forgetful of my lofty aim of doing good to Thy children. Endow me with strength of heart and mind so that both may be always ready to serve the rich and the poor, the good and the wicked, friend and enemy, and that I may never see in the patient anything else but a fellow-creature in pain.

If physicians more learned than I wish to guide and counsel me, inspire me with obedience toward the recognition of them, for the study of the science is great. It is not given to one alone to see all that others see. May I be moderate in everything except in the knowledge of this science; as far as it is concerned may I be insatiable; grant me strength and opportunity to always extend its domain; for knowledge is immense and the spirit of man can also extend infinitely, to daily enrich itself with new acquirements. To-day he can discover his errors of yesterday, and tomorrow he may obtain new light on what he thinks himself sure of to-day. O, God, Thou has appointed me to watch o'er the life and death of Thy creatures; here am I, ready for my vocation.[12]

Saladin's death in 1183 was followed by a period of internal revolt, and in the accompanying violence and confusion the Arabs turned on the Jews. To make matters worse, a plague broke out in Egypt with the result that Maimonides' attempt to minister to the stricken people night and day without rest was too much for his already weakened body. He was confined to his bed for a whole year and recuperated very slowly. It was five years before he could resume his normal life.

In the Jewish quarter of Cairo, an interesting superstition has persisted to the present day. When a person is sick and has not improved through medical means, his family takes him to the old synagogue, called Rab Moshe, to sleep for several nights in the cellar under the main prayer room of the synagogue. This is reminiscent of the *incubatio* of ancient Greek sanitariums like that of Aesculapius, where patients slept in the sacred precincts of the temple to receive visitation from the god of healing; and, as in the ancient practice, not a few cures were reported through the blessing of the great prophet and physician, Maimonides. It is said that when King Fuad I of Egypt was ill in 1935, the Jews borrowed some of the king's clothes and placed them in the prayer room of the synagogue where they remained for a week. The faithful Jews believed that the improvement of the ruler's condition came through the blessing of Maimonides.[13]

[12] Max Felshin, *Moses Maimonides* (New York, Book Guild Publishers, 1956), pp. 159, 160.

[13] The practice is described by Max Meyerhof in *Essays on Mai-*

Maimonides' medical research was versatile and eclectic, but it is perhaps true that his medical writings show less originality than his philosophical and theological work. His success as a practitioner no doubt accounted in part for his fame throughout the medieval world and the widespread use of his books during the Middle Ages.[14]

The Rambam's influence in the field of medicine was as great in his time as that of Hippocrates in his era. His medical books became standard references for several centuries, and many of his observations and treatments have remained unchallenged down to the present day. In view of his preoccupation with community work, the spiritual guidance of his people, and his medical practice, it is hard for us to imagine Maimonides having any time for philosophical writing; but somehow in the midst of his multifarious activities he was able to complete his greatest literary work, the monumental *Guide for the Perplexed*.

---

monides, pp. 265, 266. He adds that "Christian and Muslim patients share the belief in the healing power of the Maimonides synagogue, and they are sometimes admitted to pass the night under the protection of his spirit."

[14] For a perceptive treatment of Maimonides as physician see Israel S. Wechsler. "Maimonides the Physician," *Menorah Journal*, Vol. 24, No. 1, Jan.–Mar., 1936, pp. 44–52.

CHAPTER SEVEN

Guide for the Perplexed

A Correspondence Course

JOSEPH IBN AKNIN went to Fostat in 1185 to study mathematics, medicine, astronomy, philosophy, and theology under Maimonides. In 1187 he moved to Aleppo, where, as we have mentioned, he engaged in a controversy with Zekarya and Samuel ben Ali. He made journeys to Bagdad and India and finally returned to Aleppo to lecture and write. He was the physician to the Emir Faris ad-din Maimun-al-Karsi and to the son of Saladin. Ibn Aknin was highly praised by Charizi and Maimonides for his poetry. In addition, he wrote several medical treatises, a commentary on the Song of Songs, and a study of Talmudic law. It appears that ibn Aknin, like his master, was a man of diverse talents.

After ibn Aknin had left Fostat and oral instruction was no longer possible, Maimonides decided to send him some lessons in philosophy which he had been preparing. These lessons were designed as a manual or guide for his friend in the problems of the Bible and religion in general. He continued to send these discourses, chapter by chapter, to his favorite pupil, and with the first installment wrote the following:

> During the entire period of our companionship, I made it my business to explain to you every thought about which you might have had some doubt. But since God has seen fit to separate us, I have made up my mind to carry out a project which I have had under consideration for a long time. These chapters are the result. They are prepared for you and for the very few who are equal to you in intelligence.

This correspondence course turned out to be *The Guide for the Perplexed*, written in the Arabic language but with Hebrew characters, and intended, as he wrote, for "thinkers whose scientific studies have brought them into conflict with religion. When I find the road narrow," he continues, "and can see no other way of teaching a well-established truth except by pleasing one intelligent man and displeasing ten thousand fools, I prefer to address myself to the one man and to take no notice whatever of the condemnation of the multitude." What was written for one reader, or a few sophisticated scholars, became one of the most influential documents in the history of Western thought.

The Uses of Reason

Maimonides' purpose in writing the *Guide* was the same as in his previous works; namely, to harmonize faith and reason, religion and science, physics and metaphysics. He reiterated that the book was only for those who had had a proper training in theology, philosophy, and logic and for those who were intellectually mature. He intimated that even those scholars would have to read with great care and not reveal the teachings to others. The truth is that the *Guide*, although ostensibly a rational explanation of biblical secrets, is an esoteric book in itself. As Leo Strauss says, in order to interpret it the modern scholar would not only be presumptuous but would have to be "endowed with all the qualities of a Platonic philosopher-king." [1] Esotericism and historicism being mutually exclusive, the modern historically conscious interpreter can only be baffled by some of the passages.

In his Introduction, Maimonides implies that the Jews had

[1] *Essays on Maimonides*, Salo W. Baron, ed. (New York, Columbia University Press, 1941), p. 56.

always been philosophers but "had lost or had been deprived of their metaphysics and science by barbarians who deprived us of our possessions, put an end to our science and literature, killed our wise men, and thus we have become ignorant." This view was held by Philo, but the claim that philosophy was an integral part of ancient Hebrew thought belongs to the realm of legend and assumes, for instance, that Solomon was a sage and wrote the *Proverbs*. The *Wisdom Literature*, consisting of the *Song of Songs, Proverbs, Ecclesiastes*, and *Sirach*, was written after 300 B.C.E. and owes its existence to the contact of the Diaspora Jews with Greek learning in Alexandria. This was not metaphysics but a prudential or utilitarian form of wisdom, a philosophy of life. The Jews of the biblical period were a people of religion, not philosophy. That is their distinguishing characteristic. The philosophical interest of the Jewish scholars of Moorish Spain, including Maimonides, can be explained only on the background of the importation of Aristotelian thought through the Arab Renaissance.

The *leit motif* of *The Guide for the Perplexed* is the application of reason to the Bible and religion. In pursuing this objective Maimonides came no nearer to empirical, objective truth than Aquinas did in his *Summa Theologiae*. Both used the rational method *within* a presupposed truth. In the case of Aquinas, it was the assumption that the Augustinian theology of the Catholic Church was universally true; and "reason" was employed through the dialectic or syllogistic method to prove the validity of the tenets; but the flaw in this reasoning was that the major premise was often questionable or false. With Maimonides, the Bible was assumed to be true, and reason took the form of allegorical interpretation in order, as it were, to save the Scripture. Wherever a biblical passage was obviously untenable or conflicted with his philosophy, he interpreted it allegorically, claiming that the words should not be taken literally but that they had an esoteric meaning. In this way he found nothing but reasonable truth in the Bible.[2] "Those passages in the Bible," writes Maimonides, "which, in their literal sense, contain statements that can be refuted by proof, can and must be interpreted otherwise. Certain passages must either be allegorical or pronounced false. The Law is perfectly true when properly understood." This kind of exegesis is arbitrary and places the author on the defensive. Maimonides justifies his esoteric interpretation on the grounds that "the Word of God was designed for all men," for simple believers and sophisticated scholars, and thus calls for two levels of interpretation—reason and faith. Where the passage manifestly defies reason, it must be taken as having a secret meaning. In this respect, the *Guide* may be considered an interpretation of the secrets of the Bible, which were hidden by parables and symbolic words. Maimonides thus sees the Bible as an esoteric book.

Maimonides, however, was less deductive in his method than the Mutakallimun who started from arbitrary assumptions which they tried to validate by the Law. Maimonides aimed to start with propositions which were "in accord with the nature of things," although, from a modern point of view, his allegorical method, as we have shown, makes less impressive his claim to objectivity.[3]

The reconciliation of the biblical text with reason by way

[2] Spinoza was highly critical of this method and called it "naïve, harmful, absurd."

[3] See Leo Strauss, "The Literary Character of the Guide for the Perplexed," article in *Essays on Maimonides*, Salo W. Baron, ed. (New York, Columbia University Press, 1941), p. 39.

of allegory was the method of the Alexandrian School in the second and third centuries and was, to be sure, an improvement over the literal view. And it is precisely the exegetical method resorted to by quasi-liberal theologians of the present day who are understandably reluctant to admit that many biblical passages are prescientific errors, primitive ideas, or outright legends. Whenever and wherever the allegorical method has been used, it has been at the expense of the historical, critical approach and has operated under the assumption that the Scripture is a unified and sacrosanct revelation of God. The weakness of this exegesis is that it presupposes a subtlety and sophistication on the part of ancient writers that can hardly be expected. When a man writing in Palestine 2,500 years ago told the story of a miracle, he believed it literally because his primitive intellectual frame of reference gave him no reason for thinking otherwise.

In other matters, Maimonides takes the scientific position that there are no miracles. Law, not caprice, regulates the universe. We must take the immutable laws of the physical world as they are and accommodate ourselves to them. Generally, he was free of preconceptions and subjective interpretation. He was courageous enough at times to differ with Aristotle, the infallible authority of the Schoolmen, and in spite of the obsolete character of some of the problems dealt with in the *Guide*, it must be said that the book has a universal quality that appeals to the modern mind.

The Nature of God

Having critically examined Maimonides' method, we now turn to the content of his masterpiece. The first two sections deal with the nature and existence of God. The order of these two subjects—the nature of God preceding the question of his existence—would seem to be in reverse, but this was because Maimonides was writing for people who had no doubts about the existence of God, who were firm in their faith but were perplexed about the expressions used in the Scripture to describe God. This illogical order, then, was deliberate. He first discusses the divine attributes or qualities of God. Here he is concerned with the problem: if God is incorporeal and purely spiritual, how account for the anthropomorphisms of the Bible? One of the telling criticisms of Moslem scholars was that the corporeal attributes of God, so profusely employed in the Bible, debased the conception of God. The answer of historicism to this objection would be to acknowledge that the Hebrew Bible is not a book but a diverse collection of books, composed over a period of eight hundred years, by many authors; that the earlier books represent primitive ideas and later books are more refined in their conception of Deity. Such an evolutionary view, involving a knowledge of the various strata in the Scripture, is not to be expected in Maimonides' time, although ibn Ezra, an early contemporary, approximated it.

Maimonides' method of interpreting anthropomorphic descriptions of God is based on the use of "homonyms." The term refers to words having two meanings: one spiritual, the other, physical. The passages in which God is represented as having physical attributes are to be taken metaphorically. For those who can think only in physical terms, or in images, such passages must be taken literally; but for the more learned minds, these terms are purely figurative. They refer to spiritual conceptions, something beyond the literal meaning, a connotation appreciated only by the initiated. When the

Bible refers to God's hearing or seeing, for example, the words are used in a spiritual rather than physical sense; they are crude images used to convey abstract ideas.

But in the mind of Maimonides even the spiritual interpretation was inadequate in describing the essence of God. The noblest qualities ascribed to God in the Bible are ineffectual approximations of his reality. God, says the author of the *Guide*, possesses none of the qualities ascribed to him. He is as far above man and his comprehension as man is above the animal. Man can think only in images, but God is beyond all images. "Praise be to Him, the all-comprehending incomprehensible Father of the Universe. When we try to behold his splendor, our vision is blinded with excessive light. When we attempt to measure his power, our knowledge becomes ignorance. When we endeavor to describe his love, our language is but the prattling of children." [4]

The God of Maimonides, unencumbered by anthropomorphisms, mythology, intermediaries, and representations, is remote and intangible. The incorporeality of God taught by the Rambam is one of the distinctive marks of the Jewish religion today. One does not even write or speak the divine name. As in the Islamic worship, this absence of representational elements and theological involvement with man affords both a sense of relief and an awareness of the eternal—a feeling expressed by Edmund Wilson:

> Thus if the outlook of Judaism seems somewhat bleak, if its observances—to a non-Jew—mean little, some contact with it is nonetheless bracing. We are living with God in an empty room—in a room without pictures: the synagogue, where the only things displayed on the walls are words. These words

[4] The unknowableness of God, the "totally Other," is characteristic of Barthianism and recent theological trends.

declare the power of the spirit, the authority of the moral sense. The source of this power and authority gains dignity from not being seen, from not being given a name, being communicated with—not through the bread and wine of Christ's flesh and blood—but only through thought and prayer. There is only the conviction of its eternal reality, and sometimes of its actual presence.[5]

Maimonides' conception of God as indefinable, unknown, and unknowable is pertinent to the current "God is dead" controversy and the revisionist theology. In their zeal to counteract heresy, the early Christians formulated Christological creeds that were too rigid and dogmatic. In like manner, the Christians' God was too anthropomorphically defined—seen as the God working in history, having predetermined all things, the omniscient and omnipotent God who is therefore responsible for all the tragedy and sin as well as all the joy and virtue in the world, the biblical transcendent God who created the world in six days and now controls its laws, the invisible Superman, the self-existent Prime Mover, the World Ground, the activating force, and Ground of Being. Today there is a noticeable shift of emphasis to existential meaning: not to what and who is God, but what is the meaning of *man's* existence. With this shift God ceases to be the Judge of Michelangelo's *Last Judgment* or the Thunderer of Mount Sinai but the still small voice within, the inner murmurings of the heart. The new attitude among Protestant theologians may well result in an honest and reverent spirit of metaphysical agnosticism akin to that of Maimonides. Even Thomas Aquinas, probably influenced by Maimonides, admitted that "we cannot know what God is, but rather what he is not."

[5] Edmund Wilson, *A Piece of My Mind* (New York, Farrar, Straus and Cudahy, 1956), pp. 106, 107.

We cannot describe God, according to Maimonides—attributes being inapplicable—but we know he exists. The ontological argument for the existence of God revolves around the problem of the creation of the world. Here, Maimonides parted company with Aristotle, who held that the world is eternal, that there was no beginning. Time and motion, he taught, are eternal and the universe was always the same; matter is indestructible but it takes on different forms; the universe was willed by God but it has always existed. Maimonides' refutation of this theory was based on scientific and philosophical grounds as well as on biblical testimony. The biblical view was that God created everything out of nothing, including time and motion, for neither could have existed without a world. Plato maintained that the world originated in time but it was not made out of nothing. Matter existed beforehand and was used by God to create the world. The gist of Maimonides' argument against the eternity of the world was that the world was willed by God. It came into existence not through mechanical causation but through the will of an intelligent Being, acting with thought and purpose. Our senses, reason, and the phenomena of nature, says Maimonides, prove that "the mind of God conceived the world and the power of God created it." The movements of the stars and the movements of the human mind, the macrocosm and the microcosm, indicate intelligence rather than blind laws. An eternal world implies mechanism and mechanism rules out life and change. The deliberate creation of the world by God, according to Maimonides, provides an answer to the question of miracles which violate law, the purpose of God in history, and the teleological principle; but mechanistic causation leaves such questions unanswered. Moreover, mechanical necessity as the governing principle of the universe would exclude the free will of man.

The passing of seven hundred years since the time of Maimonides throws a different light on his arguments. For one thing, modern thinkers would insist that the universe is run according to immutable law. The best scientists today might use the term "cosmic consciousness" for God, if they were theists; or "universal law," if they were nontheistic; in any case, they would take their stand upon the inviolability of natural law and man's function to adjust to that law—and in this view they would have the support of Maimonides' successor, Spinoza. The principle of uniformity and predictability in physical law is an accepted axiom of our day, and every scientific discovery confirms it.

Spinoza's theory of cosmic necessity was a form of theism bordering on pantheism: the physical universe is the body of God and the laws of the universe are the mind of God. His belief in the immutability of these laws resulted in the idea of a closed universe which precluded free will on the part of man. The will of God as seen in the unchangeable laws of nature is unrelated to the desires, reactions, and attitudes of men and to their ideas of ugliness or beauty, adversity or benevolence. Man is a product of environment and is chained to his destiny. He is merely a cog in a cosmic machine.

On the other hand, the rejection of eternalism and mechanism and the corresponding acceptance of God's willful action in time carried with it for Maimonides the implication of free will. Intelligent purpose on the part of the Creator implies the same on the part of the created. Within the framework of certain restrictions due to the mental and physical capacity of the individual and to the laws of the natural world, man in his daily life is free to choose. His actions are not predetermined except in the above-mentioned manner. To be sure, circumstance may influence the decision, but it is man who makes the decision. It must be conceded that man is born with certain tendencies and as he grows he develops a certain kind of temperament which elicits this or that kind of action. But in spite of a person's predilection to intemperance or cowardice or impulsiveness, he can by self-discipline acquire the virtues of moderation, courage, and emotional maturity. Man can decide to perform a certain act; he can also decide against it. Without will there can be no ethics because the moral life hinges completely on choice between good and evil. If man's conduct is predetermined, there is no sense in the Ten Commandments or the moral demands of the prophets, for without freedom such exhortations to morality are meaningless. Without freedom it would be useless to strive to be a success in a certain profession if one were destined to enter another. If man's actions are not of his own choice, it is unreasonable to punish or blame the murderer. (Strangely enough, this is precisely the point to which social psychology and psychiatry have led our courts in their dealings with criminals who, they say, are, in almost every instance, sick, insane, or irresponsible.) Strict determinism is a *reductio ad absurdum*, and undermines morality and religion.

Maimonides spoils his own argument at this point by saying that "nothing man does is accidental; God foresees all our thoughts and actions." The critical point is that while He may foresee them he cannot change them, for if the divine economy does not permit the free choice of the person, he is not a person. The essence of personality is the possession of thought, feeling, and will. God cannot intervene in the process of history, violate his own laws of nature, or overrule the will of man; otherwise, nature would be unreliable and God, a capricious tyrant.

Elsewhere Maimonides modifies his view of God's providence by conceding that "God has endowed man with reason, with the power to choose between right and wrong." He who uses this gift to do evil thereby removes himself from the source of all goodness and alienates himself from God. God's attitude is constant; it is one of outgoing love and forgiveness, but man decides whether to move toward God or away from him. The Jewish prophet of Nazareth gave the best illustration of that teaching in his story of the Prodigal Son.

It appears that Maimonides, more prophet than philosopher, tries to hold God's supervision of man's thought and action in one hand and man's freedom in the other; at least, he does insist on man's power to choose and, in doing so, escapes the fatalism of the modern determinists.

The Problem of Evil

The next topic discussed in the *Guide* is the perennial problem of evil.[6] Having already supported the doctrine of the freedom of the will, Maimonides would naturally be expected to take that principle as his cue. His approach, however, was from an entirely different direction. It was the argument of extreme monism: God is unified; all that exists is a part of the mind of God. Since God is all-powerful, omniscient, and perfect, and has created all things, it follows that the world is good; there can be nothing evil in it. This is the answer of Stoicism and of modern Christian Science. Those who take a more empirical view would contend that evil is objectively

[6] See *Guide*, III, pp. 10–12.

real. Maimonides' reply to this would be that what we call evil is a negative element—the absence of good. Matter is nonexistent. Evil is simply the negation of the positive or the good; it is a privation, just as darkness is the absence of light, poverty, the absence of wealth, and sickness, the absence of health. Evil is not a fact but the absence of fact.

The relegation of matter to a formless entity has persisted in philosophical monism; but the idea of the nonexistence of floods, droughts, earthquakes, cancer, blindness, and arterial sclerosis is more than the realist can take. These evils are real and if God did not cause them, they are, in every instance, the direct effect of a physical cause. The physical laws that bring about such evils operate independently of God's will; or to put it in a larger framework, they are involved in the total economy of the universe and are consistent with law even though they affect man adversely. Maimonides would probably have agreed with this reasoning, for he later sets aside his negative definition of evil and falls back upon the two causes of evil: the mutability of nature and the possession by man of free will. Life, he says, has a beginning and an end. A life implies mutability which is a part of God's plan. Transitions result in evil, an indispensable ingredient of life. Such physical evils as earthquakes, epidemics, and disease are inherent in the world of nature because of the destructibility of matter.

Concerning the problem of evil and the nature of God, Maimonides' interpretation of the book of Job as found in the *Guide* (Part III) proceeds axiomatically on the premise that man's suffering is a result of sin, but he follows with a novel qualification. If man in the exercise of free will chooses to violate God's laws, the evil consequence of the choice is inevitable. "Wrong cannot be ascribed to God. . . . All evils and afflictions, as well as all kinds of happiness, whether they concern an individual person or a community, are distributed according to justice, but affliction does not come from God as a testing." Approaching the problem from a purely philosophical point of view, he sees the biblical parable of Job as a drama of a man seeking wisdom and truth. It is true, he says, that those who suffer are guilty of iniquity. This means logically that Job, who suffers much affliction, was sinful, but the point is clearly made in the story that Job was righteous. Job's anguish was spiritual. The physical adversity was unimportant, so that in his new revelation of God he finds wisdom and is vindicated. External affliction is not an evidence of God's disfavor and proof of sinfulness. The criterion for righteousness with Job is an internal awareness of God's presence. Evil is a rejection of God. The physical world of pain is secondary.[7] This view is consistent with Maimonides' overriding principle that the intellectual is superior to physical and even moral excellence. Theoretical knowledge is the only true perfection—the knowledge of God's love and justice.

Maimonides attributes human or moral evil to the deliberate choice of man. The acts of injustice, cruelty, and violence perpetuated by one man against another or one group against another are willed. Evil also results from human passion and greed. The inordinate desire for money, the intemperate appetite for food or sexual pleasure leads to sin. Man injures his body by excess and his mind by perversity. It is within the power of men to overcome or avoid such evils by curbing

[7] For a discussion of Maimonides' treatment of the book of Job see H. Joel Laks, "The Enigma of Job," article in the *Journal of Biblical Literature*, Vol. 83, Part IV, pp. 345–364.

their desires and disciplining their minds. If a person can be satisfied with life's necessities, he will find happiness, for such things are easy to find.

Divine Communication

In connection with communication between God and man Maimonides next discusses the nature of prophecy.[8] He regards prophecy as a human acquirement as much as a divine gift. It is a communication from God but is available to those exceptional people who achieve the requisite mental and moral maturity. It is an insight into truth gained by the cultivation of the imagination and the intellect to the point where there is direct perception. This shortcut, bypassing rational and sense experience, is akin to the modern, western view of mysticism in which the mystic is so attuned to the divine intellect that he penetrates intuitively the spiritual world. Prophetic insight, says Maimonides, is possible only in those individuals who are morally and physically sound and who have sufficiently developed their imagination and spiritual wisdom. It goes without saying that a person with evil thoughts or an untrained mind could never aspire to prophecy. It does not follow, however, that given these human achievements, prophecy is always possible. It is still a divine gift depending upon the will of God. It seems, therefore, that Maimonides was trying to reconcile two opposing views of prophecy. One theory held that prophecy was purely a gift conferred by God, who could bestow it even on an ignorant person if he was morally perfect. The other view was that only the highly trained person could qualify, that while the prophet was a messenger of God, he became one by virtue of his character and his intellect. Maimonides, combining the two views,

[8] *Guide*, II, pp. 32–48.

emphasized the prerequisites of intelligence, goodness, and imagination, but claimed also that prophecy was limited to those who were spiritually in harmony with the mind of God. From among such would God choose his messengers.

The message of the prophet, Maimonides explains, is often couched in figurative language. He describes his experience of God in the form of a vision or dream which is not to be taken literally but parabolically. Moses was the greatest of the prophets and his prophecy was different in kind from that of other seers. The genius of Moses was supernatural. He received the Torah from God, a unique revelation which is incapable of improvement and is truth written for all time.

In Maimonides' concluding topic, the Law, he sees the climax of divine communication.[9] The Law is man's guide to action; it is God's plan for man's perfection. Every law has a specific purpose and satisfies a definite human need. Some laws, particularly the ceremonial precepts, appeared to have no meaning. Some authorities claimed that there was no need to search for a meaning because the sole reason for their existence was the will of God. They thought that to attribute a rational explanation to these laws would reduce them to the status of mere human institutions. Like many people to-day who confuse obscurity with profundity, they saw in the very irrationality of these laws proof of their divine origin. Maimonides was rationalist enough not to agree with this naïve belief and argued that although the purpose of certain laws may not always be clear, there is a reason back of every precept.

The Law has a twofold purpose: the improvement of the body and the improvement of the soul. Biblical law can be divided into four main categories: (1) precepts embodying

[9] *Guide*, III, pp. 25–50.

beliefs in the nature of God, (2) moral and social provisions, (3) historical and genealogical material, and (4) ceremonial requirements. Maimonides' explanation of the last group does not take into account the hygienic and physiological conception of holiness which was formulated by Ezekiel and the authors of the "Priestly" and "Holiness" Codes. His theory regarding sacrifices precipitated a controversy when he justified the continuance of sacrificial rites on the grounds that men are used to this form of worship and God would not command his people to discontinue something that was natural to them. This rationalization was rejected by his critics who recognized that some legal precedents are related to a certain period but are irrelevant to later periods.

Reception of the Guide

For many bewildered minds the *Guide* was the work of a saintly prophet, smoothing out for them the road through the rocky ravines of doubt and confusion and leading them to the inspiring heights of Sinai. But to others it was the work of the devil, a heretical document of the first order. Progressive Jewish scholars, particularly those with a philosophical approach, saw in the *Guide* a much-needed fusion of Greek rationalism and Hebrew piety. Conservative rabbis everywhere took umbrage at the Rambam's theism which denied the corporeality of God and pictured the Deity as a purely spiritual entity. They clung to the thundering God of Sinai, a physical, personal Being, and saw the book as a further factor in the secularization of Judaism and the disappearance of the Hebrew tradition. Rabbi Salomo ben Abraham of Montpellier in France placed a ban on the writings of Maimonides on penalty of excommunication. He was joined in this condemnation by several leading French rabbis. Salomo's decree, aimed chiefly at the *Mishneh Torah* and *Guide for the Perplexed*, resulted in counter-excommunications by followers of Maimonides. The rabbis of Lunel condemned the followers of Salomo. Europe was split into two camps—the Maimonists and the anti-Maimonists.[10]

The controversy took on a more serious aspect when some of the liberals, following the implications of Maimonides' rationalism, extended their case by claiming that the entire Torah was allegorical, much of the Scripture unhistorical, and God a spiritual incorporeal Being. They also found in the *Guide* justification of their nonobservance of some of the traditional laws. The Fundamentalists took their stand on a firm belief in the Torah as a divine revelation, the entire Scripture as historically valid, and God as corporeal. The modernists among the Jews of France were undoubtedly influenced by the Albigenses, a heretical Christian sect which flourished in Provence during this period. Some of the more militant critics of the *Guide* prevailed upon the Catholic Church to take action, with the result that the Dominicans banned and burned Maimonides' books and persecuted his followers. Some of the well-known rabbis who joined the opposition to Maimonides and his writings were Meir of Toledo, Samson of Sens, and Daniel of Damascus. The last named was later excommunicated by David, the Exilarch of Damascus. The extremists among the Maimonists, angered by the campaign against their leader, were equally guilty in their intolerant treatment of the anti-Maimonists.

The controversy aroused the indignation of many fair-minded rabbis. Abraham ben Chasdai appealed to French Jews to cease "this inhuman perfidy" and repent of their sins. It was a disgrace, he said, to calumniate a great man like Mai-

[10] See pp. 127–131.

monides and equally atrocious to excommunicate the anti-Maimonists. He was joined by the scholar Samuel Saporta who condemned both extreme parties.

The dissension finally subsided, but it reappeared some fifty years later in a more violent manner, the outcome of which was the banning of all philosophical and scientific study throughout French Jewry. Learning was restricted to the Talmud and the Bible. This was clearly a setback for the Maimonists and liberal Jews. But just as the two sides were about to join battle they were caught up in a larger catastrophe in which the altercation over religious and secular study was forgotten. On July 22, 1306, the Jews were expelled from France, and all their property was confiscated. The one concern of escaping alive united all Jews, and in their common distress they fell back upon the wisdom and guidance of Maimonides.

In the century that followed the appearance of the *Guide* much of the opposition disappeared and it emerged as "the philosophical Bible of the Jews." It inspired many other books, most of which were interpretations and commentaries. *More Hamore* (a Guide for the *Guide*), written by Shemtob Falquera, included not only an exposition of the Rambam's teachings but dealt also with criticisms of the *Guide*. Another disciple of Maimonides, the Spanish philosopher Joseph Kaspi, brought out a twofold interpretation: one for the philosopher and another for the layman. Acting on the conviction that the *Guide* could be read with profit by "the perplexed of all nations and religions," Moses Narbone wrote a book in which he tried to relate the *Guide* not only to Greek philosophy but to Moslem science and Christian ethics.

It was logical that Maimonides' friend, Samuel ibn Tibbon, should make the first translation of the *Guide* in Hebrew.

In his request, Maimonides advised Tibbon to "render the thought rather than the words" (a good suggestion for any translator). "Do not bother to follow the order of the sentences too slavishly," he wrote. "Examine each passage as a whole; see that you thoroughly understand it; and then rewrite it in your own words. If you find it necessary to omit or to add certain phrases, do not hesitate to do so." The Rambam continued with the admonition that the translator should be familiar with Greek philosophy, particularly Aristotle, for "he was the greatest thinker in history just as Moses was the greatest prophet." The translation was all that Maimonides had hoped it would be. As the standard Hebrew edition, it brought into the language a new philosophical vocabulary and permanently enriched Jewish thought. In its original Arabic form it exerted a profound influence in Moslem circles. The *Guide* was translated into Latin in the thirteenth century and into Italian in the sixteenth.[11]

Viewing the *Guide* critically and from the vantage point of our own day, we can discern certain shortcomings; but they are the shortcomings of the times. No author, writing in the twelfth century—however great a prophet he might have been—can be expected to possess the intellectual criteria of the nineteenth or twentieth century. Maimonides, like Aquinas, was unable, for instance, to transcend Aristotle; whereas

[11] For a detailed analysis of Maimonides' sources see Shlomo Pines. *The Guide of the Perplexed* (Chicago, University of Chicago Press, 1963), pp. lvii–cxxxiv. This edition, with translation by Pines and critical introduction by Leo Strauss, is based on the Arabic text established by S. Munk (*Le Guide des Egarés;* 3 vols. Paris, 1856–66) and edited with variant readings from Isachar Joel (*Dalat al-Hairin,* Jerusalem, 1930–31). Unfortunately it contains no titles, chapter headings, or subheads. Like all ancient manuscripts, the original had no paragraphing, no capitalization, and little punctuation.

Spinoza, five centuries later, writing on the background of the Renaissance, the science of Galileo and Copernicus and the philosophy of Bacon, could cast aside the Aristotelian shackles that had bound the medieval mind. Maimonides lacked a knowledge of comparative religion and the history of religions that philosophers of a later era were to possess. Thus, he sees Moses as differing in kind from the rest of humanity, a demigod, the instrument for the revelation of the divine Law. He pictures God as a respecter of persons, concerned with a particular people. In holding to the uncritical view of the Mosaic authorship of the Pentateuch, Maimonides ignored the testimony of the text itself which repeatedly deals with post-Mosaic times. In spite of his emphatic denial of corporeality in God, he sees God as a person giving the Torah (written in Hebrew!) to Moses on Mount Sinai.

The *Guide* can hardly be considered to be philosophy in the strict sense of the word. It is concerned with philosophy as related to Jewish theology and biblical tradition. Maimonides' intention was to preserve the sanctity of the Scripture at all costs; he therefore resorted to the esoteric interpretation in those passages where literalism was manifestly impossible. Thus the genealogical tables in Genesis serve to point out a moral lesson; and the flood story emphasizes the truth that God is a just judge who rewards the righteous and punishes the wicked. Such forced interpretation is accomplished at the expense of a worthy conception of God. Inconsistencies in the *Guide* are frequent. In one place Maimonides asserts the nonexistence of matter, but in another context he says that evil is caused by the mutability of nature and the deterioration of matter. In one connection he is deterministic, but in another he holds vigorously to free will. On the one hand, he claims that God is completely unknowable; on the other, that God communicates with man. Inconsistency, however, is the privilege of genius, for the same phenomenon is found in Voltaire, Bacon, and Emerson.

Maimonides' labored use of allegory and lack of the historical sense cannot detract from the total impact of the book on medieval Jewry and on all later religious and philosophical thought. It is the spirit of the man that outweighs the letter. His physics and his metaphysics may prove to be inadequate for us but his teaching that true religion must be intellectually respectable as well as spiritually inspiring and that loving God is of no worth without personal moral integrity—this teaching is eternally relevant and stamps its author as one of the greatest prophets in history.

CHAPTER EIGHT

Thinker and Doer

The Aristocracy of Learning

THE COMPLETION OF THE *Guide* was the climax of Maimonides' career. The remaining fourteen years were given to correspondence, medical practice as physician to the court, public service as *Nagid*, and private devotion to his family. These activities were carried on in spite of broken health and political troubles. The period following the death of Saladin was filled with dissension in the government. The Rambam had much to do with the restoration of order and the formulation of equitable laws affecting labor and economic life.

Maimonides' conception of society was based on the aristocracy of learning in which the scholar occupied the top rung on the ladder of civic life. As the most important citizen, the man of learning, according to Maimonides, should be given respect and be subsidized by the government in his research. The scholar should not regard his learning as a means of gaining a livelihood but as a labor of love. On the other hand, he felt that the scholar should have an occupation of some kind and devote part of his time to it. In his own case it was his medical practice and, to a lesser degree, the jewelry business. Spinoza, it will be recalled, ground lenses for a living, and in ancient times Jewish scholars invariably had some form of employment.

Men of learning, Maimonides held, should not mingle with the common people (Am ha-Arez) even in religious ceremonies. The learned ones, of course, must prove worthy of this prestige by their exemplary conduct, their cleanliness, and neatness in dress. They must be cultivated and genteel and, in their dealings with others, kind and gracious. His idea of aristocracy pertained only to learning and never to inherited wealth or high position. There should always be the opportunity for an ambitious person of the lower classes to attain a better place in life through education. After a student had completed his studies he could participate in city government and community life.

Maimonides was accused of being both aristocratic to the point of snobbery and intolerance and also politically ambitious. That he tried to curry favor at the court and played up to those who had the power, as Abd al-Latif, a Bagdad physician, claimed, is an unfounded accusation, but there is no doubt that he affected at times an air of superiority in his writings. In the *Guide* and in some of his letters Maimonides adopts a boastful and arrogant attitude—a manner of writing often encountered in the Middle Ages and the Renaissance period. His conceit is unmistakable in the *Guide* where, in several places, he makes it clear that he wrote the book only for a philosophical clique; else he would be casting pearls before swine. On the other hand, it must be recalled, he wrote the *Mishneh Torah* for laymen. He often spoke contemptuously of the ignorant; then again he was generous with his time and was sympathetic in his attitude toward the common people. He was greatly concerned with introducing new laws for the improvement of the condition of slaves and always taught that they were human beings and should never be humiliated or cruelly treated. In the "labor-management" problem he said the worker was morally obligated to do an honest day's work but should be treated like a free man.

Maimonides regarded marriage and family life as the focal point of society, but felt that a man should not marry unless he was gainfully employed. Oddly enough, he thought that marriage among relatives was preferable because it was conducive to understanding and congeniality, and even recommended marriage between uncle and niece.

He believed in a system of social welfare in which the community supported its poor. A weekly collection should be made and distributed among the needy. A board would decide which cases were most in need of help. Charity played an important role in medieval Jewish life, but according to Maimonides it should not be dispensed so as to embarrass the recipient. "Maimonides' charity," wrote Menahem ben Zerach, "extended to all men. His letters of consolation strengthened the minds of his unfortunate contemporaries, and his material aid sustained their bodies." His home was a refuge for the poor and the sick. "The way to heaven," said the Rambam, "is paved, not with holy words, but with worthy deeds; the way to love God is to serve one's fellowman."

Maimonides set down a list of eight degrees in giving alms, each one being an improvement on the former in merit:

1. Those who bestow charity but with grumbling.
2. Those who do so cheerfully but give less than they ought.
3. Those who contribute only when they are asked and what they are asked.
4. Those who give before they are requested to do so.
5. Those who give charity but do not know who benefits by it, although the recipient is aware from whom he has received it.
6. Those who give charity and do not disclose their names to those who have received it.
7. Those who do not know to whom their contribution

will be given while the recipients do not know from whom they have received it.

8. Those who extend a loan or bestow a gift upon the needy, or who take a poor man into partnership or help him to establish himself in business so that he should not be compelled to apply for charity. Such people practise the highest degree of charity.[1]

Maimonides was an aristocrat of the mind. Like the Renaissance humanist, Erasmus, he brought clarity to everything he touched. He judged all previous knowledge in the light of reason and relevance; and his own formulation of the truth was orderly, logical, and sane. His philosophy was not of the abstruse or pedantic type but always pragmatic, for his interest was only in the enhancement of human life.

Lest it be supposed that Maimonides was without personal flaws, it must be observed that, also like Erasmus, he had some of the defects of the intellectual genius. He had no ear for music and apparently disliked poetry; at any rate, he made room for neither in his world. Both partook too much of sentimentality and thus, in his mind, both were a form of mental intoxication, dulling the rational faculty. Although some of his writings had a poetical quality and became a part of synagogue ritual, he thought poetry was "a waste of time." There was no place in his life for play. He had never been young. Wine, women, and song were equally alien. In this respect he differed greatly from his contemporaries, for ibn Ezra had praised in verse the relaxation of games; Halevi had extolled the ecstasy of love; and Gabirol had sung of the pleasures of wine. To Maimonides the banquet table was a sign of decadence, a moral weakness.

[1] This condensed version of the eight classes of charity is quoted from Solomon Zeitlin, *Maimonides: A Biography* (New York, Bloch Publishing Company, 1955), p. 139.

The penalty of the purely rational outlook on life is a numbing of the imagination, a stifling of the aesthetic sense. Erasmus, for instance, could walk through Switzerland and not see the snow-capped mountains above his head or the tiny edelweiss beneath his feet. Maimonides, likewise, seems to have had no time "to stand and stare" and lacked the child-like sense of wonder at the world of art and natural beauty. What went through his mind at the sight of the pyramids under whose shadow he lived for so many years? Did he ever stop to contemplate the nature of the civilization that produced these mountains of Ra, these houses of eternity, that were standing fifteen hundred years before the time of Moses? His letters and writings give us no clue.

His rule of moderation was applied also to the use of language. He shunned extravagant and mawkish phraseology as inimical to the accurate presentation of truth. Words should be employed with thrift and used only in the furtherance of science.

Philosophy of Life

In their eternal relevance the moral maxims of Maimonides rank with the wise sayings of Ptah Hotep, Francis Bacon, and Benjamin Franklin. The following aphorisms from the *Guide* and the *Responsa* speak for themselves:

When I have a difficult subject before me—when I find the road narrow, and can see no other way of teaching a well-established truth except by pleasing one intelligent man and displeasing ten thousand fools—I prefer to address myself to the one man and to take no notice whatever of the condemnation of the multitude.

The fact that a certain proposition has been proved by a dialectical argument will never induce me to accept that proposition, but, on the contrary, will weaken my faith in it and cause me to doubt it. For when we understand the fallacy of a proof, our faith in the proposition itself is shaken.

Do not consider a thing as proof because you find it written in books; for just as a liar will deceive with his tongue, he will not be deterred from doing the same thing with his pen. They are utter fools who accept a thing as convincing proof because it is in writing.

The truth of a thing does not become greater by its frequent repetition, nor is it lessened by lack of repetition.

The wise man is a greater asset to a nation than is a king.

Let the truth and right by which you are apparently the loser be preferable to you to the falsehood and wrong by which you are apparently the gainer.

It is of great advantage that man should know his station, and not erroneously imagine that the whole Universe exists only for him.

It is to be feared that those who become great in riches and comfort generally fall into the vices of insolence and haughtiness, and abandon all good principles.

It is in the nature of man to strive to gain money and to increase it; and his great desire to add to his wealth and honour is the chief source of misery for man.

When we continually see an object, however sublime it may be, our regard for that object will be lessened, and the impression we have received of it will be weakened.

These adages reveal the ethical pragmatist. What is of greater importance, however, is the fact that his precepts were found not only on paper but in his life. He practiced what he preached. "In all our actions," he said, "we must observe the Golden Mean. The virtuous life is the moderate life. To this rule there is only one exception. There must be no moderation in our humility." Maimonides himself was a truly humble person, always ready to learn from others, even his own students. He scorned the quest for fame and notoriety. He disliked controversy and when he found it necessary to engage in polemics he usually omitted his opponent's name. On the other hand, he cited the names of other people whenever he was in agreement with them. His objective was to prove the validity of an idea through rational means rather than win a victory over an opponent. He was calm in the face of insult and personal attacks. Restraint of anger and avoidance of revenge were not only the right ethical attitude toward others but were conducive to mental and physical health.

In his dealings with others Maimonides lived above the legalistic world. Love was greater than law and righteousness was more to be desired than rules.

Mention has been made of Maimonides' adherence to the Aristotelian doctrine of the Golden Mean. This he applied to all aspects of daily life and human relations. He was particularly opposed to asceticism as practiced by Christian hermits and anchorites. Such extremism he regarded as a form of spiritual sickness. Religion, he said, is the aggressive life lived in the community among people rather than a withdrawal from society to the desert.

> The well-being of the body . . . is anterior in nature and time. The latter object is required first because the well-being of the soul can only be attained after that of the body has been secured; for a person that is suffering from great hunger, thirst, heat or cold, cannot grasp an idea even if communicated by others, much less can he arrive at it by means of his own reasoning. But when a person is in possession of the first perfection, then he may possibly acquire the second perfection, which is undoubtedly of a superior kind and is alone the source of eternal life.[2]

[2] *Guide*, III, p. 27.

Although Maimonides saw the Jewish religion as a revelation from God, he did not regard it as the only revelation of truth. He recognized the common scriptural background of Islam and Judaism and did not consider the forced conversion of the Anusim as apostasy nor the worship of true Moslems as idolatry. In spite of widespread persecution of Jews by Christians he maintained an attitude of tolerance toward them. He refused to call the Karaites heretics and worked for their reclamation.

Maimonides' rational outlook and belief in freedom compelled him to reject astrology as an absurd and unreasonable belief and as inconsistent with freedom of the will, a stand which he took in spite of biblical and Talmudic recognition of it. One should not capitulate to fatalism simply because some sage or ancient prophet held that a person's destiny was determined by the star under which he was born. "It is true," he writes, "that you may find stray utterances in the Rabbinical literature which imply a belief in the potency of the stars at a man's nativity, but no one is justified in surrendering his own rational opinions because this or that sage erred or because an allegorical remark is expressed literally." In his plea for common sense in this matter, he said: "Man must never throw his understanding behind him." Human thought and action are self-willed and are in no way connected with the heavens. He would have agreed with Shakespeare's Cassius: "The fault, dear Brutus, is not in our stars but in ourselves, that we are underlings." Man's fate is not sealed; he makes or mars his own life. The fatalistic belief in astrology reduces man to an automaton, robbed of all moral decision. There can be neither merit nor blame in a world of determinism. In a letter to the Jews of Marseilles he said that works on astrology were the product of foolish men who had no scientific knowledge. In this letter he clearly distinguished between astrology and astronomy, and in that distinction Maimonides showed himself to be genuinely modern. "Astronomy is a science through the study of which we learn the movements of the planets and the moon in their orbits."

Maimonides was no less vigorously opposed to superstitious ideas such as belief in omens, taboos, fetishes, and signs. These "knock-wood" practices have been continued more or less seriously from the Middle Ages to the present day. As to the use of the *mezuzah* which was placed on the doorpost of the house, he held that rather than being a fetish or good luck amulet it was a symbol of the presence of God in the house and an observance of the commandment to keep the Law "on the doorpost of your house and on your gates" (Deuteronomy 6:9).

Divine Providence and Human Will

As a cosmic theist, Maimonides conceived of God as Supreme Intelligence, a metaphysical entity. Men must approach God with "morality and piety but also with philosophical understanding." [3] His theism was neither mystical nor emotional but rational. It was a spiritual monotheism, but one based on reason rather than feeling. To philosophical Personalists today, this view of God would appear to be too impersonal, too abstract; it is a case of philosophy corrupting theology, an exaltation of abstract intelligence at the expense of the biblical or moral conception of God. One spokesman for the Personalistic School sees this view of God as an illustration of "the pitfalls and perils of the philosophical approach to religion" and concludes that with Maimonides "the biblical

[3] Yellin and Abrahams, *Maimonides* (Philadelphia, Jewish Publication Society of America, 1936), p. 193.

God is rationalized into a metaphysical principle." [4] To this it might be replied that rather than being a pitfall or defect, Maimonides' definition of God as incorporeal and without attributes has real meaning for our Space Age. No longer can we believe in a God who intervenes in history, who causes people to act cruelly or unreasonably, who is the sole property of a particular religious group, or a respecter of person. "God," wrote the Rambam, "is the Ultimate Form, the Final Purpose, the End of Ends," the intelligent primal cause, the world ground.[5]

It follows from Maimonides' transcendent view of God as "das ganz Andere" that he held God's mind to be vastly different from the mind of man:

> . . . The sum total of the idea I am trying here briefly to explain is the following: we cannot apprehend the true nature of God's essence; yet we know that His existence is the most perfect, without any admixture of imperfection or change or affection in any way. Similarly, though we do not know the true nature of God's knowledge, because it is His substance, yet we know that He does not sometimes apprehend and at other times remain unaware, i.e. that He never acquires new knowledge; also, that His knowledge is not of a multiple nature, nor finite; that nothing of all existing things is hidden from Him, and that His knowledge of them does not change their nature, but the possible retains its nature as a possibility. Anything in this enumeration that appears contradictory, is so only owing to the structure of our knowledge, which has nothing in common with His knowledge except the name.

[4] Lowell M. Atkinson, "Maimonides," an article in *Religion and Life*, Vol. 22, No. 1, Winter 1952–53, p. 130.

[5] The "God is dead" movement in contemporary theology is a belated recognition of the inadequate and irrelevant conception of God held by pseudoliberal Protestants.

Regarding the relation of divine omniscience to human will, Maimonides explains that God's overall knowledge of man's action does not imply that man's will is predetermined by reason of God's knowledge. In that case, laws, commandments, and human decision would be meaningless. God's knowledge does not in any way affect man's moral responsibility and free choice. The following excerpt from the *Mishneh Torah* presents a cogent argument for free will and the rejection of determinism:

Free will is bestowed on every human being. If he desires to turn toward the good path and be just, he has the power to do so. If he wishes to turn toward the evil path and be wicked, he is at liberty to do so. And thus it is written in the Torah, "Behold, the man is become as one of us, to know good and evil" (Gen. 3:22)—which means that the human species stands alone in the world—there being no other kind like him as regards this subject of being able of his own accord, by his reason and thought to know what is good and what is evil, with none to prevent him from either doing good or evil . . .

Let not the notion, expressed by the foolish among other peoples and most of the senseless folk among Israelites, pass through your mind that at the beginning of a person's existence, the Only One, blessed be he, decrees that he is to be just or wicked. This is not so. Every human being may become righteous like Moses, our teacher, or wicked like Jeroboam; wise or foolish, merciful or cruel; niggardly or generous; and so with all other qualities. There is no one that coerces him or decrees what he is to do, or draws him to either of the two ways; but every person turns to the way which he desires, with the consent of his mind and of his own volition. Thus Jeremiah said, "Out of the mouth of the Most High, proceedeth not evil and good" (Lam. 3:38); that is to say, the Creator does not decree either that a man shall be good or wicked.

Accordingly it follows that it is the sinner who has inflicted harm on himself. He should, therefore, weep for, and bewail what he has done to his soul—how he has mistreated it. This is expressed in the next verse, "Wherefore doth a living man complain, or a strong man? Because of his sins" (Lam. 3:39). The prophet continues: Since liberty of action is in our hands and we have, of our free will, committed all these evils, it behooves us to return in a spirit of repentance: "Let us search and try our ways, and return to the Lord" (Lam. 3:40).

As to human perfectability, Maimonides in the *Guide* lists four types of moral excellence attainable by man:

The first and lowest is the one for which the inhabitants of the earth destroy each other, i.e. the perfection of wealth. It comprises the property, clothes, instruments, slaves, lands and such like which a man owns. . . . This is a perfection which has no real connection of any kind with that person, but only a relation. The pleasure derived from it is in any event for the most part purely imaginary, i.e. the pleasure of saying: this is my house, this is my slave, or this property is mine, this is my army. If he were to look at himself he would discover that all this is outside his own self and that every single one of these possessions exists on its own account. Therefore, as soon as the relation ceases, that individual, who was a powerful king, may one bright morning find that there is no difference between him and the lowliest of mankind, though no change has occurred in any of those things that stood in a relation to him. The philosopher shows that he who devotes his energy and efforts to the acquisition of this kind of perfection strives for something purely imaginary, for it is a thing which has no permanence. Even if the wealth remains in his possession throughout his life, no perfection in his own self will ever result from it.

The second kind of perfection is more closely connected with man's own self. This is the perfection of physique and appearance, as when a man's constitution is perfectly balanced and his limbs and organs are in proper proportion and of the requisite strength. This kind of perfection is also not considered to be a final purpose, because it is physical perfection which is given to man not insofar as he is human, but insofar as he is animal, and he shares it with the lowest beasts. Moreover, if a man were to reach the utmost degree of strength possible for him, it would not be equal to that of a strong mule, not to speak of that of a lion or an elephant . . .

The third kind of perfection affects the substance of the person more deeply than the second. It is the perfection of ethical virtues. . . . Most religious prescriptions are designed for the attainment of this kind of perfection. This kind of perfection is, however, merely a prerequisite to something else, not a purpose in itself, because all ethical qualities refer to relations between a person and others. In a way this perfection in a man's ethical qualities is nothing but a prerequisite for the benefit of society. It thus becomes an instrument for something else. Just suppose that a man is all alone and has no business with anyone: in that case all his ethical qualities will be found to be vain and void. There would in such a case be no need of them and they would in no way contribute to his personal perfection. It is only with regard to others that man needs them and receives any benefit from them.

The fourth kind of perfection is true human perfection; that is, the attainment of rational virtues. By this I mean, of course, the conception of ideas which lead to correct opinions on metaphysical matters. This is the ultimate purpose, and this is the one which bestows upon man true perfection, being peculiar to him alone. It brings him eternal life, and by it man is man. Consider each one of the preceding types of perfection, and you will discover that they belong to others, not to yourself—or if you must needs have it according to the conventional view, they belong to you and others at the same time. This last perfection, however, belongs to yourself exclusively, and no one else has any share in it.[6]

The question of immortality and the doctrine of the resurrection loomed large in medieval Judaism as it had among the ancient Pharisees. Maimonides had included in his *Commentary on the Mishneh*, as the last item in the Thirteen Articles, a statement of belief in the resurrection of the dead. At that time, it appears, he referred to the survival of the soul rather than the body—a spiritual view of the resurrection. As Zeitlin shows, he followed the Pharisaic interpretation that the soul was freed of the body after death and enjoyed immortality.[7] Later, in his letter, *Techiyath Hamethim* (The Resurrection of the Dead), written at the request of his pupil, Joseph ibn Aknin, he hedged on his former position by allowing for the possible resurrection of the soul in the body. Still later, he accepted the idea of the resurrection of the body itself, but could not determine its time. The special treatise of Maimonides on the resurrection (Maqala) was written in response to a critical essay by Samuel ben Ali, criticizing his eschatological views.[8] His final thought was that physical resurrection is scientifically impossible as a violation of natural law; nevertheless he included it as a part of his theological system by assigning it to the realm of miracle. Such a stand is disappointing to the modern reader but was probably a concession made under pressure in the same way that many religious leaders

[6] *Guide*, III, p. 54.

[7] Solomon Zeitlin, *Maimonides: A Biography* (New York, Bloch, 1955), p. 150.

[8] For a critical analysis of this document, see Joshua Finkel, "Maimonides' Treatise on Resurrection, a Comparative Study," an article in *Essays on Maimonides*, Salo W. Baron, ed. (New York, Columbia University Press, 1941), pp. 93-121.

today do not dare state publicly all their private views. He was unequivocal, however, on the immortality of the soul as "acquired intellect" not dependent upon the body. This also fails to satisfy the liberal thinker of the present day. In spite of equivocations, however, Maimonides was the only thinker up to his time daring enough to affirm the incorporeality of ultimate existence.

On Economics

As Salo W. Baron observes, it is remarkable that the Jewish people, who became a predominantly mercantile group in the Middle Ages, never produced an economist "to lend theoretical formulation to the existing reality." [9] Maimonides himself, in spite of his preoccupation with Jewish jurisprudence, did not evince any interest in economic theory. His only treatment of the subject was under "domestic economy," a subdivision of practical philosophy or political science. His writing in this category had to do with those precepts "by which the head of the household knows how the members are to help one another and how they are to be provided for in the best possible way in accordance with the requirements of a given time and place." [10] As for secular economic laws, Maimonides repeatedly asserts in the *Guide* and elsewhere that "the true law, beside which there is no other, viz. the Law of our teacher, Moses, is the only guide to spiritual and physical perfection." In other words, the Torah provides all one needs to know in his social and economic life.

It is not to be supposed, on the other hand, that the claim to exclusiveness on the part of the Torah as the law of life

[9] "The Economic Views of Maimonides," in *Essays on Maimonides*, pp. 127–264.
[10] *Treatise on Logic*, Ch. 14.

and the rejection of the idea of an independent science of economics ruled out the recognition of the reality of the economic world. Maimonides in fact devotes a large part of the Code to economic matters. In this document he discusses charities, loans, gifts, damages, crime, and civil law. But for him the authority in these matters was the Torah and the Talmud and not the Arabic and Aristotelian social philosophy. Apparently in this instance, he considered the Aristotelian system inadequate or perhaps dangerous to the nonpolitical theocracy of medieval Judaism. Maimonides, while recognizing the necessity of earning a livelihood, always subordinated physical and monetary interests to the well-being of the soul. "The desire for excessive wealth and property can be inimical to the higher morality, destructive to the ordeal of the people and the government of the household." One of the objectives of the perfect law is to "remove the desires, to disparage them and to reduce them to the absolute minimum. Most of the damages done to people in the various states arises from the lust for money and its accumulation and the excessive desire to increase possessions and honors." [11]

Such a philosophy as this might have led to otherworldliness and a life of withdrawal, but Maimonides' thought was not antisocial. He did say that the scholar must be a man set apart, aloof from the marketplace, but he recognized the wisdom of an organized society and the necessity of social responsibility. "Men engaged in such transactions must not refrain from mutual assistance in order to promote their common interest; neither of the parties must strive to increase only his own profit and that he alone should enjoy the whole benefit of the transaction."

[11] *Guide*, III, pp. 33, 39, 42.

Civil and political legislation is necessary for the preservation of social justice and the prevention of crime. Laws must be enacted which will "remove violence among men; that is to say, that no one shall be guided in his actions by his likes and dislikes or by his power to act, but that everyone shall constantly do what is good for the common welfare." [12] Maimonides' social theory included the moral obligation of each individual to interfere when he sees a wrong being done. "He who can protect and does not do so is himself guilty of the transgression." Maimonides' urban orientation and residence in Cairo, where trade and commerce were the basic means of livelihood, made it inevitable that his theory of social responsibility should be applied to private enterprise. In this he was not inhibited by the anticommercial tradition of the medieval Christian church. He saw that business was just as important as agriculture but recognized the necessity of adapting the traditional ethical standards to trade so that the public interest might be served. "Since financial cooperation is necessary for the people of every city, it is impossible to have these transactions without a proper standard of equity and without useful regulation." [13] In the matter of weights and measurements, for instance, Maimonides insisted on the civil and judicial control of their manufacture as well as periodic examination. Supervisors, he said, should be appointed in every city to inspect scales and measures in all stores. Anyone found using measures below the standard size should be subject to fine or punishment. The Jewish communal authorities should fix prices in order to prevent excessive profits and the local

[12] *Guide*, I, p. 46; III, p. 27.
[13] *Guide*, III, pp. 3, 35.

leaders should also agree upon the rate of profit for the community.[14]

The economic views of Maimonides can be seen as an attempt to preserve an equilibrium between the traditional Talmudic ordinances and the changing practices of the times. To a great extent the Talmudic law was adaptable to his age, thus producing a proper balance between the public interest and the rights of the individual. This adjustment of Jewish tradition to the real world of the twelfth century helped the Jewish people to preserve their continuity and, at the same time, their identity.

On the Bible

In evaluating Maimonides' views on the Scripture it is imperative to bear in mind his century and the strictly orthodox Jewish background as over against, for instance, the comparatively enlightened age of Spinoza. As the recognized leader of world Jewry, Maimonides was trying to reconcile the faith of the fathers with the new rationalism and at the same time keep the people loyal to the teachings of Judaism. He was on this account compelled to adapt and compromise in order to hold his people together. Spinoza, on the other hand, not being responsible for any group, was a free lance, disowned by his own people, and therefore had a detached and independent outlook on everything. The Jewish feeling about the Scripture had varied not at all in the millenium that followed the canonization at Jamnia (90 C.E.). The Law

[14] For a more technical discussion of Maimonides' economic theories, particularly regarding money and banking, slavery and free labor, see Salo W. Baron, "The Economic Views of Maimonides," in *Essays on Maimonides*, pp. 127–264.

and the Prophets were the unique revelation from God and could never be changed. The Jews became the "People of the Book." It was all they had to hold them together in their never-ending exile. Not having a national state, they had to find in the Bible their source of cohesiveness and destiny. The Mosaic law and the Talmud had to be adapted to the changing times. This made for a strict continuation of the legalism of Ezra. The life of medieval Jews was controlled completely by Pentateuchal law, the *Mishnah*, and the *Gemara* as they were repeatedly recodified.

As new intellectual forces developed, fresh accommodations of Jewish law had to be made. It was in the confrontation with the Arab renaissance of the twelfth century that Maimonides developed a theory of biblical interpretation that would leave Judaism intact in that changing world. It is surprising that with Maimonides' all-encompassing work he did not undertake a commentary on the Bible, at least the Pentateuch. What Pentateuchal exegesis we have from him is to be found mainly in *The Guide for the Perplexed*.

His theory, as we have previously observed, was based on the assumption that everything in the Bible is inspired and therefore true. (This criterion is precisely the opposite from that of Spinoza, who said that the Bible is inspired only insofar as it is true.) All depends, said Maimonides, on the interpretation: if a given passage conflicts with reason, it is the interpretation that is wrong. The passage is then to be interpreted figuratively. The fact that the Bible was written for both the learned and the unlearned necessitates this dual exegesis. There are many passages which cannot be understood by the untrained reader either because he lacks the philosophical knowledge or the intellectual capacity, in which case he has to be satisfied with the literal meaning. The danger of this situation, according to Maimonides, is that to take such a passage literally will often result in a fallacious conception of God. To accept literally the anthropomorphic descriptions of Deity which occur in the Bible is tantamount to idolatry. Such passages, he explains, are metaphorical expressions, as are descriptions of the creation and Ezekiel's picture of the divine chariot. This is the essence of Maimonides' rationalism as applied to Scripture, and it is based on the a priori assumption that the Bible contains nothing contrary to reason. Any apparent discrepancy must be interpreted figuratively.

We must also remember that in the twelfth century there was no such thing as Textual Criticism and the Septuagint was virtually unknown.[15] The Masoretic text, with all its variant readings was considered inerrant.[16] Contradictions, double traditions, anachronisms, and inconsistencies were either ignored or interpreted allegorically. The Pentateuchal references to the death of Moses, to the occupation of Canaan, and to the kings of Israel did not alter the belief in Mosaic authorship! The only Jewish scholar of this period who questioned the unity of the Pentateuch was Abraham ibn Ezra, who, as we have elsewhere observed, with his historical point of view, was the one great exception in medieval times.[17] The principles of Hebrew grammar and the meaning of Arabic words were used in the interpretation of the Bible, but such aids did not in any way affect the tendentious exegesis of Scripture. (For that matter, even a Fundamentalist theologian today, operating with all the latest textual apparatus, can and

[15] Textual Criticism: the comparative study of manuscript differences; Septuagint: Greek version of the Old Testament.

[16] Masoretic text: the standard Hebrew text from the tenth century.

[17] It must be noted that Hivi al Balki (ninth century?) had thrown doubt on the unity and Mosaic authorship of the Pentateuch.

does hold to the divinely inspired and infallible nature of the Bible.) Such is the danger of the a priori principle in philosophy and theology.

The allegorical interpretation of narrative material was not difficult, but to find an esoteric meaning in traditional laws and institutions was a different matter. The observance of sacrifices, for instance, as found in the Scripture, could hardly be interpreted as allegory. The temple, the priests, and the sacrifice were very real and were centered in the ancient Hebrew worship. Sacrifices also contradicted Maimonides' philosophical conception of God. He solved the problem by saying that, like other ancient peoples, the Hebrews under Moses were accustomed to offering sacrifices. To prohibit the practice suddenly would be too serious a break in tradition; so Moses allowed them to continue the custom with the condition that they make their offerings only to their God. Ultimately, he hoped, they would discontinue the sacrifices.[18]

[18] *Guide*, III, pp. 29–32.

Maimonides and Later Thinkers

The Impact on Jewish Thought

THE IMMEDIATE EFFECT of the philosophy of Maimonides was a cleavage in the Jewish world. European Jewry was divided into two camps, Maimonists and anti-Maimonists, both of which exaggerated their differences and at times became violent antagonists. For the one party Maimonides was the complete embodiment of truth; for the other, he was the arch-heretic. Excommunications and book burnings were common occurrences. The net result of this bifurcation, however, was beneficial to Judaism. It was only a temporary division and in the end the resultant compromise produced more balance in Jewish thought. The Maimonist emphasis on reason succeeded in giving to the Jewish religion a philosophical character while the effect of the anti-Maimonist thought kept Judaism from being lost in pure rationalism. Further, the Cabbalistic influence supplied a mystical aspect which Maimonidean thought lacked. But here also it was the influence of Maimonides that kept Judaism from becoming a predominantly esoteric religion. The most significant element in Maimonides' thinking was his antagonism to the anthropomorphic conception of God, a theological point of view which accentuated the spiritual quality of Judaism.

The Maimonist–anti-Maimonist controversy was particularly severe in France and Spain while the Rambam was still living. In Provence the liberal wing of Judaism had already felt the influence of the Albigenses, the heretical Christian sect. Aristotelianism and rationalism had also taken root in this region, with the result that there was strong support of Maimonides from such teachers as Jonathan of Lunel. When Meir Abulafia of Toledo, Spain, wrote a letter to the Jews in Lunel, caustically criticizing Maimonides' views on the resurrection and the incorporeality of God, he was publicly rebuked by Rabbis Aaron and Sheshet of Barcelona, who defended the Rambam's belief in the spiritual nature of the resurrection, explaining that the Talmudic interpretation as physical was only a concession to the uneducated masses who were incapable of comprehending the purely spiritual view.

Other prominent critics of Maimonides were Abraham ben David Rabad of Provence, Rabbi Samson of Sens, and Rabbi Daniel of Damascus, a pupil of Samuel ben Ali of Bagdad. Hostilities mounted when excommunications were issued by Rabbi Solomon of Montpellier, an influential literalist, against all who studied the *Mishneh Torah* or secular works of any kind. Such actions only precipitated countermeasures. The liberals, following the implications of Maimonides' philosophy and, perhaps, going far beyond it, attempted to form a left-wing party in Judaism. They interpreted the Torah allegorically and ignored Jewish ritualistic laws. The followers of Solomon, on the other hand, regarded the Bible as literally inspired, obeyed all Jewish regulations and precepts in every detail, and held strictly to the corporeality of God.

When the Inquisition of Innocent III liquidated the Albigenses in the second decade of the thirteenth century, the intellectual climate of Southern France changed. The Dominicans, coming into power, made it their business to stamp out all heresy and liberal thought. This change moved French Jewry toward a conservative position and gave added influence to fundamentalist Rabbi Solomon. Reverberations were

felt in Spain, where Jewish scientists in Saragossa, reacting to Solomon's excommunications, had a counter-excommunication issued against him and his followers.

In the midst of all this discussion in France and Spain several rabbis tried to pour oil on the troubled waters. One was Nahmanides (1194–1270), who had received a letter from Meir Abulafia defending Solomon's attack on Maimonides and urging that Solomon be given an opportunity to present his case. Nahmanides yielded to this request and sent letters to various Jewish leaders urging them to withhold their judgment. At the same time, Spanish Maimonists called upon their representative David Kimhi to visit Judah al Fakhir, an influential court physician, and persuade him to take action against Solomon. Kimhi's request was not only denied but he himself was attacked by Judah as a heretic. Judah, furthermore, gave Solomon and his students his blessing as preservers of the true religion of Judaism. Judah's action was obviously prompted by the fear of a split within Judaism. The radicals had gone too far in their rejection of Jewish precepts and in their relegation of the Torah to pure allegory. For the sake of unity and in order to hold the common people, it was expedient, he thought, to follow the conservatism of Solomon. He himself disagreed with Maimonides' philosophical approach and the use of allegorical interpretation. Also he resented the popular reverence for Maimonides as even greater than the prophets.

Kimhi's reply to Judah was extremely conciliatory but the latter persisted in his view that the *Moreh Nebuchim* was alien to Jewish tradition and that adherence to the Torah and the Jewish precepts should not be contaminated by Greek thought. He blamed Jewish radicalism in France as the cause of persecution by the church.

Nahmanides made a second attempt at reconciliation by exonerating Maimonides of heresy, by endorsing his philosophical interpretation of Judaism, and by praising the *Mishneh Torah* which taught the incorporeality of God. He advised the rabbis of France to give up their opposition to philosophy and to cease combating heresy by force or law.

Rabbi Solomon's next move was to enlist the aid of the Catholic authorities in France in banning *The Guide for the Perplexed.* The Council of Sens and the papal legate had already prohibited the reading of Aristotle on penalty of excommunication. Now when Solomon made clear that the *Guide* was thoroughly Aristotelian, the Dominican and Franciscan authorities put a ban on the *Guide* and burned all the copies that could be found. This act of intolerance infuriated the Jews, including those who had sided with Solomon, and prompted Kimhi to appeal once more to Judah al Fakhir, who stood practically alone among the rabbis in support of Solomon, but he failed to act.

Those leaders who, like Joseph of Burgos, in Spain, tried to conciliate the two parties, pointed out that Solomon was within his rights in criticizing the *Guide* and his fear of a schism was justified. The radical Jews were responsible for the bitter controversy in both France and Spain. Joseph regarded Maimonides as the greatest scholar since the compilers of the Talmud, but it should be understood, he said, that the *Guide* was written only for scholars and students and not for the uneducated.

The dispute continued in France and Spain. The books of Maimonides and the entire Talmud were publicly burned in Paris in 1142. Church authorities joined anti-Maimonists in banning the works of Aristotle. Excommunications issued by both factions were common. The prohibition of scientific study by the chief rabbi of Barcelona was counteracted by a ban on anyone who hindered students from studying philosophy or science. The controversy over the writings of Maimonides continued into the nineteenth century. Its persistence confirmed Maimonides' own fear that parts of the *Guide* would be misinterpreted. His opponents uniformly ignored his discriminating and critical acceptance of Aristotle, his reverence for the Torah as supreme authority, and his insistence that the Talmud should never be supplanted.

Recognition of the Maimonist–anti-Maimonist controversy, however, should not blind us to the ever-increasing influence of Maimonides upon Jewish thinkers from the thirteenth century onward. As we have said, the cleavage did not really disrupt the unity of Judaism. Ultimately liberals and conservatives alike regarded the *Code* and the *Guide* as containing the authoritative principles of the Jewish faith. As far as rabbinical law is concerned, the *Misneh Torah* had more influence than the *Guide* and became the prime authority of Jewish law and, in the minds of many rabbinical leaders, was held as an infallible document. Philosophers like Mendelssohn, mystical Cabbalists, nationalistic Zionists, ultraconservative Rabbinists—all quoted Maimonides as their inspiration. Solomon Maimon (1754–1800), the German philosopher, was such an admirer of the Rambam that he adopted his name and wrote: "My reverence for this great teacher went so far that I regarded him as my ideal of the perfect man. I looked upon his teachings as if they had been inspired with divine wisdom itself." [1]

The attachment of the Cabbalists to Maimonides was a surprising development in view of their antirationalist and

[1] David Yellin and Israel Abrahams, *Maimonides* (Philadelphia, Jewish Publication Society of America, 1936), p. 215.

mystical outlook on life. Naturally, they ignored his appeal
to reason in their fantastic flights of imagination. The self-
appointed Messiah, Abraham Abulafia, who tried to convert
Pope Martin IV to Judaism, was a follower of Maimonides
and tried to equate the *Guide* with the mysteries of the Cabbala. Shemtob ibn Gaon claimed that Maimonides had himself
become a Cabbalist. The Cabbalists went so far as to forge
in the Rambam's name letters in which philosophy was discarded in favor of magic.

The Scholastics

The influence of Maimonides on European thought in general
and on the Scholastics in particular was due to the spread of
Aristotelian thought among the Christian theologians. The
more Scholasticism leaned toward Aristotelianism, the greater
became the need to reconcile Greek thought with that of the
Church or at least define the boundaries so as to avoid conflict. It was here that Jewish thinkers, particularly Maimonides, provided guidance.[2] We have previously referred to the
permeation of the Greek spirit in the Moslem, Jewish, and
Christian world. In the twelfth and thirteenth centuries it was
in fact difficult to distinguish Arabic, Latin, and Hebrew
writings. The first Latin translation of the *Guide* was made
from Judah al-Charizi's Hebrew version in the first part of
the thirteenth century. The influence of Maimonides on Christian thought came originally through Albertus Magnus (1193–
1280). Christian theologians also became acquainted with the
Maimonidean philosophy through the commentaries of Averroës. The Franciscan Alexander of Hales, William of Au-
vergne, and Johannes Scotus (1266–1308) were greatly in-

[2] See Jacob Guttmann, *Moses ben Maimon: Sein Leben, Seine
Werke und Sein Einfluss,* Vol. 1, p. 139.

debted to the *Guide*. The Dominicans, usually intolerant of non-Christian thought, were also attracted to Maimonides' teaching, and one of them, Vincent of Beauvais in his *Compendium of Science* paid the Rambam a glowing tribute.

The main channel through which Maimonidean philosophy passed into Scholasticism was the *Summa Theologiae* of Thomas Aquinas (1225–1275). In this *magnum opus*, which became and has remained the definitive manual of Roman Catholic theology, Aquinas followed Maimonides in his method of reconciling religious philosophy with Aristotelian logic and joining faith and reason. The point at which the thought of Aquinas and Maimonides converged was their opposition to the Aristotelian doctrine of the eternity of the universe, or to put it positively, their belief in the biblical account of creation in time. Aquinas follows Maimonides in his discussion of divine attributes, providence, prophecy, free will, and proof of the existence of God as seen in the eternity of motion. The relation of Aquinas to Maimonides is well summarized by Isaac Husik as follows:

> It is no doubt an exaggeration to say that there would have been no Aquinas if Maimonides had not preceded him, for Aquinas had access to the works of Aristotle and his Arabian commentators, the former of whom he studied more diligently than Maimonides himself. But there is no doubt that the method of harmonizing Aristotelian doctrine with traditional teaching so far as the common elements of Judaism and Christianity were concerned was suggested to Aquinas by his Jewish predecessor.[3]

[3] Isaac Husik, *A History of Medieval Jewish Philosophy* (Philadelphia, Jewish Publication Society of America, 1960), pp. 306–307. Regarding Thomas' dependence on Maimonides in his teaching on divine attributes, Guttmann writes: "Was die Lehre von den göttlichen Attributen betrifft, so stimmt Thomas mit Maimonides zunächst

Levi ben Gerson

Although practically all post-Maimonidean thought in the Jewish world took the form of a commentary on Maimonides, as Isaac Husik points out, Gerson and Crescas developed a rather independent type of thought. The latter especially departed considerably from the Rambam in rejecting the authority of Aristotle and leaning more heavily on emotion rather than reason—a contrast which recalls the Voltaire-Rousseau antithesis.

Levi ben Gerson (1288–1344), a Frenchman, was the most original thinker among all the Jewish philosophers of the thirteenth and fourteenth centuries. His philosophical writings form a connecting link between Maimonides and Spinoza. He was not only a great student of the Talmud but one of the few important medieval experts in biblical exegesis. Gerson's effectiveness, however, was hindered by his lack of knowledge of Arabic and Latin. He wrote entirely in Hebrew. He is known largely for his philosophical work *Milhamot Adonai* (*The Wars of the Lord*) in which he applied the scholastic method to the solution of theological and philosophical problems which were introduced but not completely dealt with by Maimonides. This volume—called by his orthodox opponents *The Wars Against the Lord*—deals with the immortality of the soul, prophecy, the omniscience of God, providence, the nature of the heavenly bodies, and the eternity of matter. In his discussion of omniscience he hints at the

darin überein, dass man sich die von Gott ausgesagten Attribute nicht als etwas zu dem Wesen Gottes Hinzukommendes denken dürfe, weil das gleichbedeutend wäre mit der Annahme von Accidentien, die von dem Wesen Gottes vershieden seien, was dem Begriff der Einfachheit oder der Einheit Gottes widerstritte. (*Moses ben Maimon*, Vol. 1, p. 181.

modern conception of a finite God; that is, God's lack of complete knowledge of the phenomenal world and his inability to interrupt the operation of universal law. But his fame throughout Europe stemmed more from his astronomical and mathematical treatises which were translated into Latin. Some of these treatises were attempts to disprove the Ptolemaic or geocentric theory and as such reveal Gerson as a precursor of Copernicus.

Gerson shared the general Maimonidean point of view toward philosophy and Scripture. The goal of knowledge is the perfection of man, or the process toward perfection, a spiritual state attained through the moral life and rational inquiry. Biblical law is designed to lead man into the twofold perfection of science and morality. Thus, the Pentateuch contains both specific laws of conduct and narratives which illustrate ethical principles by implication. Gerson also shares Maimonides' belief in the compatibility of reason and authority. Both were convinced that the Bible did not contain anything that was opposed to reason.

It is unnecessary to rehearse the laborious ramifications of Gerson's discussion of the nature of the intellect and the will. On the whole, he follows the Maimonidean principle that although physical law is immutable and man's life is limited by it, man can use his will and his power of choice to enable him to accommodate himself to universal law and to enhance his own life within that body of law. There is, says Gerson, such a thing as chance and not all contingencies can be foretold. In this department of thought, however, he held a more logical and less theological point of view than Maimonides. The Rambam had insisted that God's knowledge, being different from ours, includes particulars and contingencies. Gerson refutes this position by arguing that if

God's knowledge is wholly different from what man calls knowledge and if God is utterly unknowable anyway, as Maimonides held, how can we define God's knowledge? The attributes that we ascribe to God can have meaning only as they resemble the same attributes in ourselves, but in God they are nearer a state of perfection. As to particulars, God has foreknowledge of their occurrence if they are law-abiding particulars but if they are chance or contingent particulars he does not have knowledge of them. God knows only those things that are an integral part of his universal order. Such a view, according to Gerson, was compatible with Scripture and was to be considered in no way a defect in the character of God. Man's choice may alter certain contingencies or events even though this power of choice may seem to limit the activity of God. To give up the idea of contingency or chance would destroy freedom and without freedom personality cannot exist. Gerson's insistence on free will with all its risks and its apparent violation of God's omnipotence was indeed a foreshadowing of modern liberal thought.

Another problem area in which Gerson shows an advance over Maimonides and anticipates modern liberalism was that of the suffering of the righteous. Contrary to the traditional or biblical view that God rewards or punishes man according to his deeds, that God causes the pious to prosper and the wicked to suffer, Gerson argued that such a view implies that God knows particulars, a claim that he had already disproved. It implies also that if God knows and determines particulars, it follows that a man cannot be held responsible for any evil which he does. As a matter of fact, says Gerson, the wicked prosper and righteous people endure untold suffering. Evil in the form of suffering falls on the just and the unjust and occurs either from the impact of physical law upon man (earthquake) or from man's free choice of action (war). In neither case does the suffering come from God as punishment. Man's foolish actions in flying in the face of universal law will inevitably bring suffering. God does not overrule his own laws of the universe to take care of individuals, whether they are good or bad. To do so would eliminate the one prerequisite for personality in man—freedom. Man's religious goal is to cooperate with his physical environment and to learn to know God, thus perfecting both spirit and intellect. God, Gerson concludes, is the Active Intellect, the Supreme Intelligence behind and in the universe. In this idea Gerson was in agreement with Maimonides.

Crescas

The influence of Maimonides on Hasdai ben Abraham Crescas (1340–1410) is found in the element of contrast rather than continuity of thought. Crescas, a Spaniard of Barcelona, represents a return to a more spiritual and less rational type of Judaism—a system of thought quite independent of Aristotle. In this departure he stood opposed both to Maimonidean philosophy and scholasticism. The superimposition of Greek speculative thought upon a purely spiritual religion was, in his opinion, a perversion of true Judaism.

In his chief work, *Or Adonai* (*Light of the Lord*), he sees the existence of God as the basis of Judaism but he rejects Maimonides' rational proof for that existence as unnecessary. He also opposes the Rambam's belief that God is without attributes and sees a closer relation between creator and creatures. In his discussion of the problems of God's providence, omniscience, omnipotence, prophecy, freedom, and teleology, he insists that God knows all particulars including contingents. God's providence is direct and extends to individuals and all forms of life. Crescas rejects Gerson's theory that suffering is caused either by the operation of free will or physical law. He minimizes the suffering of the righteous and the well-being of the wicked in this world as being a matter of inheritance or evil as good in disguise. He sees God as a respecter of people and Israel as the special recipient of God's favor. His idea of divine providence leads naturally to God's omnipotence, which he accepts unconditionally. His insistence on the absolute omniscience and omnipotence of God automatically ruled out the typically Jewish doctrine of free will. In this he tried to have his cake and eat it too by trying to distinguish between determinism and fatalism—always a tenuous differentiation. Crescas' solution of the problem of the curtailment of man's freedom and his distinction between God's punishment of willful human acts and the absence of punishment in acts externally caused, influenced the thinking of Spinoza, whose philosophy was also dangerously close to cosmic determinism.

Crescas' antirational outlook—as opposed to Maimonides—is seen finally in his teaching on the purpose of the soul. The end of man is to love God and this is a nonintellectual function. The soul is a spiritual substance independent of the body and is therefore capable of immortality; whereas the intellect cannot grow eternally.

Spinoza

Maimonides and Einstein are separated in time by eight centuries but in thought they are not far apart and the connecting link is Baruch Spinoza (1632–1677). Maimonides' religious monotheism became Spinoza's philosophical monism, which in turn became Einstein's cosmic theism.

Spinoza's dependence on Maimonides was conclusively demonstrated by Manuel Joel (1870), who went so far as to say that the *Tractatus Theologico-Politicus* could never have been written without *The Guide for the Perplexed*. Spinoza's study of Maimonides antedated considerably the writing of the *Treatise* and the *Ethics*, so that all his later thinking was tested in the light of the principles of the *Guide*. He was influenced also by Bruno (1548–1600), whose master idea was unity, and by Descartes (1596–1650), whose mathematical approach to philosophy helped to break the grip of Scholasticism and pave the way for modern thought. "All reality," said Bruno, "is one in substance, one in cause, and this reality is God." Spinoza, amplifying this theme of Maimonides and Bruno, defined the visible universe as the "body of God" and the energy that moves the universe and the laws that govern it as the "mind of God." But mind and body are one just as matter and energy are one. God is the infinite substance of the universe; all creatures and substances partake of his essence. By "substance" Spinoza did not mean material things but "that which exists in itself and is conceived through itself, that essence of which all else is a transient mode or form." Substance does not depend on anything else for its existence. It is infinite. God is the one free, self-contained, and eternal Being on which all else depends. God is the immanent cause of the universe and constitutes the order of things.

God's creation, however, was not made to suit man's desires and intelligence. The mind of God is beyond human understanding, and it is not for finite man to judge the infinite wisdom of God. Carlyle later compared man's ignorance of God's plans to a minnow living in a brook. The minnow and the brook in which it swims are both affected by the ocean,

the winds, the clouds, and the moon but the minnow compre-
hends none of these things. He also used the analogy of the
insect, which, crawling with great difficulty over a crack in
a column of the Parthenon, has no idea of the architecture
of the building. In like manner, finite man knows nothing of
the infinitude of God's plans. God *is* the universe and its laws
cannot be set aside by the whims or petitions of man. The
laws of nature—the will of God—are not related to man's
view of them as beautiful or ugly, adverse or benevolent.

Manifestly with Spinoza there was little ground for free
will. Being an integral part of our environment, we are dependent upon natural forces, and, although we are conscious
of our acts, they are not free. We are cogs in a cosmic
machine. But every person, being a part of the universe, is
related to the whole. His one note in the symphony of life
counts; it is his contribution to the grand harmony. If the
world has not been made for him, at least, he has been made
for the world. Without his page the book of life would be
incomplete. Although man with his brief span is but a passing
phenomenon in the eternal universe and is chained to his
destiny by the necessitarian character of law, nevertheless he
has the moral responsibility of accommodating himself to the
laws of the universe in order to find satisfaction in the eternity
of which he is a part. The ends of man, according to Spinoza,
were "to understand things through their first causes; to govern the passions or acquire the habit of virtue; and to live in
safety and with a sound body. Blessedness consists in love
towards God, a love which springs from the highest kind of
knowledge. This love is virtue itself."

In the main features of Spinoza's metaphysics and ethics,
there is a clear dependence upon Maimonides. Both saw the
universe as "a totality through which alone it is possible to

know God." [4] Both conceived of immortality in a qualitative rather than a quantitative sense—"not existence for an indefinite time, but the quality of being above all time," a living of the eternal life rather than for the hope of immortality. Both taught a religion of reason and law.

It is in Spinoza's extension of Maimonides' principles that we see divergence. Maimonides, for instance, while maintaining that "God is the efficient cause of the particular events that take place in the world just as he is the efficient cause of the universe as a whole," [5] nevertheless insisted on freedom of will. The dilemma of holding to man's free will along with God's omnipotence and omniscience was resolved by either stating on the one hand that while God has foreknowledge of man's action, he does not cause it or determine it, or, on the other hand, by denying God's foreknowledge of man's choices. In any case, he saw no contradiction in holding to both God's foreknowledge and man's freedom. To Spinoza this explanation was unsatisfactory. If God does not have foreknowledge, he argued, he is not omniscient. If he has foreknowledge and omnipotence, then he is the conscious cause of every event. If man can still act freely, it follows that he can obstruct and change the determinate will of God. [6]

A comparative study of Maimonides and Spinoza leads to the conclusion that in matters theological and biblical the latter was much more independent and progressive. This is nowhere more obvious than in his theories of biblical criticism.

[4] Leon Roth, *Spinoza, Descartes and Maimonides* (New York, Russell and Russell, 1963), p. 105.

[5] *Guide*, I, p. 69.

[6] For a detailed study of the differences between the systems of Maimonides and Spinoza, see Harry A. Wolfson, *The Philosophy of Spinoza* (New York, World Publishing Company, Meridian Books, 1934), and Leon Roth, *op. cit.*

Whereas Maimonides believed that the Torah was the infallible word of God revealed to Moses, Spinoza held that the Pentateuch was composite in authorship; in fact, was partly from the hand of Ezra (fifth century B.C.E.) and, moreover, contained many anachronisms and historical errors. Maimonides' explanation of the presence of passages that clearly contradicted both reason and history was that they were to be construed allegorically. Spinoza interpreted this type of rendering as intellectually dishonest.

Spinoza's first principle of biblical criticism was that the Bible must be approached without preconceptions or prejudice and must be subjected to the same analysis as any other book. If it is to be concluded that the Bible is inspired, it would have to be the result of critical study of the text itself and not from an a priori or traditional assumption. He criticized Maimonides' method as follows:

> The opinion of Maimonides was widely different from my own. He asserted that each passage in Scripture admits of various, even contrary meanings; but that we could never be certain of any particular interpretation until we knew that the passage, as we interpreted it, contained nothing contrary to reason. If the literal interpretation clashes with reason, then, though the passage seems perfectly clear, it must be interpreted differently.[7]

We have seen that by "differently" Spinoza meant allegorically. As an example, Spinoza quotes Maimonides' allegorical interpretation of the scriptural passages which speak of God as corporeal and his literal interpretation of the biblical references to the creation of the world in time, and concludes:

[7] *Tractatus Theologico-Politicus,* trans. by R. H. M. Elives (Bohn's Libraries), p. 75.

Therefore, the method of Maimonides is clearly useless; to which we may add that it does away with all the certainty which the masses acquire by candid reading or which is gained by any other persons in any other way. In conclusion, we dismiss Maimonides' theory as harmful, useless, and absurd.[8]

Spinoza summarizes his own critical and historical method as follows:

1. We must know the nature and the properties of the language in which the books of the Bible were written and in which their authors were accustomed to speak.

2. We must make an analysis of each book and an arrangement of its contents under heads. We should also note all the passages which are ambiguous or obscure, or which are mutually contradictory.

3. We should investigate the environment of all the prophetic books extant; that is, the life, the conduct, and the studies of the author of each book, who he was, what was the occasion and the epoch of his writing, for whom did he write, and in what language. Further, we should inquire into the fate of each book; how it was first received, into whose hands it fell, how many different versions there were of it, by whose advice was it received into the Bible (canon); and lastly, how all the books now universally accepted as sacred were united into a single whole.[9]

The foregoing statement identifies Spinoza as laying the foundation of historical criticism as we know it today. He wisely concedes that due to the difficulties inherent in the

[8] *Ibid.*, pp. 86, 87.

[9] *Ibid.*, pp. 15–25. To appreciate how concisely and completely Spinoza anticipates the historical method of modern biblical critics, see my *A History of the Bible* (Boston, Beacon Press, 1959), pp. 307–309.

Hebrew language—absence of vowels, incomplete syntax—
it is impossible to gain a true and complete knowledge of the
text. "I do not hesitate to state," he continues, "that the true
meaning of Scripture is in many places inexplicable or at best,
mere guesswork." But despite this, he concludes, the things
that really matter—ethical and spiritual values—can be understood perfectly. "The precepts of true piety are expressed
in very ordinary language, and are equally simple and easily
understood. . . . Therefore, we need not be much troubled
about what remains; such matters are more curious than
profitable." [10]

This amazingly discriminating approach to the Bible has
never since been expressed in more trenchant language, and
it sets a challenging standard for present-day scholars and
laymen alike. The first prerequisite for biblical study is to
recognize that the Bible is not a scientific textbook but a collection of moral and spiritual truths. The prophets, Spinoza
observes, were not omniscient and are to be read only for the
moral guidance they provide.

Spinoza's scientific attitude is most clearly seen in his literary criticism of the Pentateuch, where he acknowledges
his debt to ibn Ezra. Mosaic authorship is rejected on the
basis of anachronisms, such as the iron bedstead mentioned in
II Samuel 12:29,30; retrospective allusions to sources later
than Moses, such as Numbers 21:14; and the presence of material that must be dated as late as the Exile. Spinoza points
out that the Pentateuch must be seen, along with Joshua and
Judges, as the work of editors and compilers, ending with
Ezra. He intimates that the Pentateuch was made up of distinct strands or documents that were later edited and calls attention to the evidences of compilation and editorial cor-

[10] *Ibid.*, pp. 65–69.

rection.[11] He places the book of Nehemiah as late as the second century B.C.E. and the publication of the book of Psalms in the time of the Second Temple. Regarding Chronicles, which is dated very late, he expresses surprise that such an unreliable book was admitted to the canon and the Wisdom of Solomon excluded. He assigns Proverbs to a post-Exilic date, denies unity to Jeremiah, regards Job as a translation of a Gentile poem, and questions the genuineness of Daniel.

Spinoza hesitated to apply his criticism to the New Testament because of his lack of knowledge of the Greek language; but he insists, at any rate, that the apostles and evangelists had no miraculous powers and wrote simply as human beings. In view of his observation of the editorial or redactional nature of Hebrew literature and his differentiation between the thought of the New Testament writers and that of a later age, it can be truly said that he stands at the threshold of the critical period in biblical study and did much to give it birth. Fearless, unprejudiced, possessing a mind at once mathematical and philosophical, Spinoza cleared away the old structures of both allegory and literalism, and then proceeded to lay a new foundation—the *Tractatus Theologico-Politicus*, which might well be called the Magna Charta of Biblical Criticism. His contribution lies in his anticipation of two successive stages that replaced the allegorical: Rationalism, or the harmonizing of the Scripture with natural law, and Historical Criticism, which assigns Scripture to its age and setting and does not try to "save" its contents. Today the rationalistic method appears as fallacious as allegory, but it was significant that Spinoza in the seventeenth century should make use of the rationalistic and prefigure the historical method.

[11] See *Tractatus* in *loc. cit.*

In recognizing the advance made by Spinoza over Maimonides in the area of biblical study, we must bear in mind the difference in time and place, for Spinoza came not only four centuries later but was writing in exile as an excommunicated heretic. (A heretic is always pushed by the opposition to positions he never would have contemplated otherwise.) The fact remains, however, that in philosophy and theology Spinoza based his *Tractatus,* as well as his rejection of the Cartesian system, on the *Guide.* The *Guide* is to be regarded as the key both to the monism of Spinoza and to much of modern European philosophy.

CHAPTER TEN

Maimonides—Our Contemporary

Eternal Relevance

FOR SEVERAL CENTURIES Maimonides was considered either as a prophet second only to Moses or as an excommunicated heretic—all depending on the prevailing intellectual climate and point of view. The verdict of time, however, is represented by the Jewish proverb: "From Moses to Moses (Mendelssohn) there arose no such man as Moses (ben Maimon)." For most Jews today the Rambam stands as a solitary figure, holding a unique place in their history, the symbol of Talmudic Judaism, the greatest Jewish thinker in the last two thousand years.

In the technical sense of the word, Maimonides, like Voltaire, can hardly be called a philosopher; but, like Voltaire, he influenced philosophical thought tremendously. Prior to the twentieth century, with the exception of Spinoza, the Jews have never produced great metaphysicians. There may be some hesitation also in calling him a theologian, for as a Jew he was not interested in dogmatics as such; but here again his ideas on the nature of God profoundly affected modern theological thought. Was he a physician? Certainly from our point of view today he was not. In his writing and instruction he added little to the medical knowledge of Galen and Hippocrates. It is unfair to judge him as a "doctor" in the light of our own times. One must guard against seeing him either as an original authority in medicine or as of no importance at all on the basis of present-day criteria. But although medicine was not his chief vocation, he became a wise and outstanding physician to the royal household and to countless common people, wrote ten books on medical science, applied common sense and reason in his practice, and stoutly opposed superstition and quackery.

It must also be admitted that much of Maimonides' output can only be regarded as obsolete today. The *Mishneh Torah* is the only book which is actually used by Rabbinical scholars. The *Guide,* as Solomon Zeitlin says, really "raised more problems in the minds of those not fully matured than it solved" and remains for the present-day scholar for the most part an intricate maze of casuistical arguments. Most of the astronomical and physical theories of Maimonides were invalidated by the Copernican revolution, but of course he cannot be criticized for not transcending the scientific knowledge of his day. On the other hand, he discarded astrology and medieval superstitions and dealt critically with Talmudic law when it was found to be opposed to science and reason. His modernism, we might say, was relative at best, but it is so in any age with any thinker. In his inability to break loose completely from the medieval bondage to Aristotle he cannot be compared to Copernicus, Galileo, and Bacon, who had several centuries of additional scientific progress behind them.

In view of the foregoing limitations, the question may be asked: Wherein consists the originality of Maimonides? What are the elements of greatness in his personality and teaching? His was not the age of specialization. He took the whole range of learning as his province. His knowledge was encyclopedic; yet he was highly discriminating in his judgment. He delved into widely separated fields of endeavor and contributed greatly to all.

For all teachers of modern Jewry—nationalist or Diaspora, humanist or ethnic, religious or secular, ethical or ritualistic

—Maimonides, with his universal spirit and doctrine of the Golden Mean, remains the wise teacher. His teaching, applied to world Jewry today, means striking a balance between nationalism and religion, not permitting the one to move toward racism or the other toward Fundamentalism. It challenges Jews with the demands of universal humanism, a wide fellowship rather than a ritualistic or ethnic isolationism.

Although Judaism possesses, probably more markedly than any other faith, a moral and spiritual accent which can and must find expression in the present and the future, like Christianity, it was born and grew up in a mythologically oriented culture. Its ancient mythology still hangs like a millstone around the neck of orthodox religion and today hinders its cultural growth in the midst of a scientifically minded society. It is here that the spirit of Maimonides can bridge that gap and free ethical Judaism from its bondage to an anachronistic legalism and help it to stand forth as a religion in which God is not the judge and lawgiver but the cosmic force in man and the universe making for righteousness, and man a co-creator and co-worker with God in this process. Torah and Talmud have been the salvation of Judaism in the past, but their literal observance today is keeping Jews from living in the twentieth century.

The Jews' stake in the infallibility of the Torah as the law of Moses automatically precludes any scholarly appraisal of the Pentateuch or purely historical approach to the Bible just as the Christological claims of orthodox Christians make impossible any genuine accord with Judaism. The modern tendency of progressive Protestant and Jewish scholars to relinquish the idea of verbal inspiration was implicit in the writings of Maimonides. The enlightened Jew can no more accept the idea that every word of the Torah was divinely inspired than an educated Protestant can believe that the New Testament is a unique revelation from the hand of God. Maimonides' statement that "the gates of interpretation are not closed" heralded the coming of nineteenth-century historical criticism.

If the Jew in America can express his distinctiveness in the prophetic values of universality, the dignity of the individual, the moral imperative, and the teleological principle, he will be perpetuating the basic ideals of democratic America. If, on the other hand, he fails in this contribution, he not only betrays his Jewish heritage but alienates himself from the mainstream of American life. The well-being of the western world desperately needs the dynamic of the Jewish genius.

The Maimonidean spirit calls for even greater concessions from orthodox Christianity. It demands that Christians cease regarding as a divine revelation the anti-Semitic teaching of the New Testament and abandon the untenable conception of Jesus, a Jew of the first century, as Deity. It condemns the theme of hate which is so prominent in the Gospels and which is later integrated into the doctrinal structure of Christianity. From the Jewish standpoint no real rapprochement can be expected as long as such dogmas and prejudices are a part of Christian thought. Ecumenical discussion can only wait upon the Christian surrender of the idea that Jesus supplanted Moses, that the New Testament replaced the Old Testament, and that Judaism is an archaic religion that served its purpose as a preparation for "the true and final religion."

Time does more than make ancient good uncouth. It makes it inadequate and sterile—a positive hindrance to progress. The task of both Judaism and Christianity today is to keep goodness alive, to meet new occasions with new insights. Time and change do not abrogate moral law, but they do demand new interpretations and applications of it. The Constitution of the United States is maintained by a process of re-interpretation by the Supreme Court, the decisions of which keep that document contemporary with the needs of the Republic. The greatness of the Constitution is its adaptability. The Torah and the Sermon on the Mount possess a like adequacy, but they must be reread in a way that challenges our times. They must be redefined, revaluated, re-experienced vitally in each generation. They must be interpreted in terms of relevant principles, rather than a set, patterned morality.

It is not in Maimonides' specific theological doctrines or scientific knowledge that his genius lies. His physics as well as his metaphysics soon became obsolete. In the perspective of history a man's greatness is measured in terms of his contemporaneousness, his eternal relevance. It is the vitality of Maimonides' spirit that is fresh today. Philosophical and theological method has changed in eight centuries, but the Rambam's ethical principles and religious attitudes are most relevant for our day. His untrammeled search for truth and wisdom, his ecumenical and tolerant spirit, the adaptability of his outlook on life to our society, his lifelong devotion to reason, and the embodiment of his principles in his own life which was spent on behalf of others—these constitute the measure of his stature. His brilliance of mind and greatness of soul enabled him to transcend time and history. Maimonides the universal man speaks to the twentieth century no less distinctly than to the thirteenth, bringing insight into the problems of both Judaism and Christianity today. It is for Christians and Jews today to be concerned with the spirit of his writings, not the letter; his ethics, not his theology; his life rather than his logic.

BIBLIOGRAPHY

Agus, Jacob Bernard, *The Meaning of Jewish History*, 2 vols. New York and London, Abelard-Schuman Ltd., 1963.

Baeck, Leo, *The Essence of Judaism.* New York, Schocken Books, 1948.

Baer, Yitzhak, *A History of the Jews in Christian Spain*, 2 vols. Philadelphia, The Jewish Publication Society, 1966.

Bamberger, Fritz, *Das System des Maimonides: Eine Analyse des More Newuchim vom Gottesbegriff aus.* Berlin, Schocken, 1935.

Baron, Salo Wittmayer (ed.), *Essays on Maimonides.* New York, Columbia University Press, 1941.

Ben-Gurion, David, *The Jews in Their Land.* New York, Doubleday, 1966.

Bokser, Ben Zion, *Judaism, Profile of a Faith.* New York, Knopf, 1963.

Code of Maimonides (Translations of the *Mishneh Torah*), 14 vols. New Haven, Yale University Press, 1949–65.

Elbogen, Ismar, *Das Leben des Rabbi Mosche ben Maimon: Aus seinen Briefen und anderen Quellen.* Berlin, 1935.

Felshin, Max, *Moses Maimonides.* New York, Book Guild Publishers, 1956.

Festschrift zur 800 Wiederkehr des Geburtstages von Moses ben Maimon. Monatsschrift für Geschichte und Wissenschaft des Judentums 79:65–207. Breslau, Marcus, 1935.

Feuer, Leon, *Jewish Literature since the Bible.* Cincinnati, Union of American Hebrew Congregations, 1942.

Fischler, Max, *What the Great Philosophers Thought about God.* Los Angeles, University Book Publishers, 1958.

Friedlander, Joseph, *Standard Book of Jewish Verse.* New York, Dodd, Mead and Company, 1917.

Glatzer, Nahum N., *The Dynamics of Emancipation: The Jew in the Modern Age.* Boston, Beacon Press, 1965.

————, *Faith and Knowledge: The Jew in the Medieval World.* Boston, Beacon Press, 1963.

————, *The Rest Is Commentary: A Source Book of Judaic Antiquity.* Boston, Beacon Press, 1961.

Glock, Charles Y., and Stark, Rodney, *Christian Beliefs and Anti-Semitism,* Vol. I. New York, Harper and Row, 1966.

Goldstein, David, *Hebrew Poems from Spain.* New York, Schocken Books, 1966.

Guttmann, Jacob (ed.), *Moses ben Maimon: Sein Leben, Seine Werke, und Sein Einfluss,* 2 vols. Leipzig, Buchhandlung Gustav Fock, 1908–1914.

Heschel, Abraham, *Maimonides: Eine Biographie.* Berlin, Reiss, 1935.

Husik, Isaac, *A History of Jewish Medieval Philosophy.* New York, Meridian Book Company, Inc., 1958.

————, "Maimonides and Spinoza on the Interpretation of the Bible," *Journal of the American Oriental Society,* No. 1, September 1935, Supplement, pp. 22–40.

Jacobs, Joseph, *Jewish Contributions to Civilization.* Philadelphia, Jewish Publication Society, 1919.

Kamen, Henry, *The Spanish Inquisition.* New York, The New American Library, 1966.

Kaplan, Mordecai M., *Judaism as a Civilization.* New York, Macmillan, 1934.

Mann, Jacob, *The Jews in Egypt and Palestine under the Fatimid Caliphs.* London, Oxford University Press, 1920–22.

Marx, Alexander, *Moses Maimonides.* Maimonides Octocentennial Series, No. 2. New York, Maimonides Octocentennial Comm., 1935.

Menuhin, Moshe, *The Decadence of Judaism in Our Time,* New York, Exposition Press, 1965.

Meyerhof, Max, "Medieval Jewish Physicians in the Near East." *Isis,* Vol. 28 (1938), pp. 432–60.

Münz, J., *Maimonides: The Story of His Life and Genius.* Boston, Winchell-Thomas, 1935.

Prinz, Joachim, *The Dilemma of the Modern Jew*. Boston, Little, Brown and Company, 1962.

Sachar, Abram L., *A History of the Jews*. New York, Knopf, 1953.

Sarachek, Joseph, *Faith and Reason: The Conflict over the Rationalism of Maimonides*. Williamsport, Bayard Press, 1935.

Schaub, Edward L., "Maimonides: His Background and His Role in History." *Monist*, Vol. XLV, July 1935, No. 2, pp. 220–23.

Sklare, Marshall, *The Jews: Social Patterns of an American Group*. New York, Free Press, 1958.

Wechsler, Israel, "Maimonides the Physician." *The Menorah Journal*. Vol. 24, No. 1, Jan.–Mar. 1936, pp. 44–54.

Wolf, A., "The Rationalism of Maimonides." *The Philosopher*, 13:150–53, October 1935.

Yellin, David, and Abrahams, Israel, *Maimonides*. Philadelphia, Jewish Publication Society, 1936.

Zeitlin, Solomon, *Maimonides: A Biography*. New York, Bloch, 1955.

Index